On God

J. KRISHNAMURTI

KRISHNAMURTI FOUNDATION INDIA

Sources and acknowledgements can be found on page 157.

Series editor   : Mary Cadogan
Associate editors : Ray McCoy and David Skitt

© —1992 Krishnamurti Foundation Trust Ltd.
      Krishnamurti Foundation of America

Published, under licence, by

Krishnamurti Foundation India
Vasanta Vihar, 64 Greenways Road
Chennai - 600 028.
E-mail: kfihq@md2.vsnl.net.in

First Indian edition 1999

ISBN 81-87326-10-7
Philosophy / Religion

Cover photo : F.Grohe
Cover design : Deepa Kamath

Printed by

The Indcom Press
44 Arya Gowda Road
West Mambalam
Chennai - 600 033.

But there is a sacredness that is not of thought, nor of a feeling resuscitated by thought. It is not recognizable by thought nor can it be utilized by thought. Thought cannot formulate it. But there is a sacredness, untouched by any symbol or word. It is not communicable. It is a fact.

Krishnamurti's Notebook, *28 June 1961*

Contents

Contents

Foreword

JIDDU KRISHNAMURTI was born in India in 1895 and, at the age of thirteen, taken up by the Theosophical Society, which considered him to be the vehicle for the 'world teacher' whose advent it had been proclaiming. Krishnamurti was soon to emerge as a powerful, uncompromising, and unclassifiable teacher, whose talks and writings were not linked to any specific religion and were neither of the East nor the West but for the whole world. Firmly repudiating the messianic image, in 1929 he dramatically dissolved the large and monied organization that had been built around him and declared truth to be 'a pathless land', which could not be approached by any formalized religion, philosophy, or sect.

For the rest of his life he insistently rejected the guru status that others tried to foist upon him. He continued to attract large audiences throughout the world but claimed no authority, wanted no disciples, and spoke always as one individual to another. At the core of his teaching was the realization that fundamental changes in society can be brought about only by a transformation of individual consciousness. The need for self-knowledge and an understanding of the restrictive, separative influences of religious and nationalistic conditionings, was constantly stressed. Krishnamurti pointed always to the urgent need for openness, for that 'vast space in the brain in which there is unimaginable energy'. This seems to have been the wellspring of his own creativity and the key to his catalytic impact on such a wide variety of people.

He continued to speak all over the world until he died in 1986 at the age of ninety. His talks and dialogues, journals and letters have been collected into more than sixty books. From that vast body of teachings this series of theme books has been compiled. Each book focuses on an issue that has particular relevance to and urgency in our daily lives.

Bombay, 6 January 1960

THE MIND IS the known—the known being that which has been experienced. With that measure, we try to know the unknown. But the known can obviously never know the unknown; it can know only what it has experienced, what it has been taught, what it has gathered. Can the mind see the truth of its own incapacity to know the unknown?

Surely if I see very clearly that my mind cannot know the unknown, there is absolute quietness. If I feel that I can capture the unknown with the capacities of the known, I make a lot of noise; I talk, I reject, I choose, I try to find a way to it. But if the mind realizes its own absolute incapacity to know the unknown, if it perceives that it cannot take a single step towards the unknown, then what happens? Then the mind becomes utterly silent. It is not in despair; it is no longer *seeking* anything.

The movement of search can only be from the known to the known, and all that the mind can do is to be aware that this movement will never uncover the unknown. Any movement on the part of the known is still within the field of the known. That is the only thing I have to perceive; that is the only thing the mind has to realize. Then, without any stimulation, without any purpose, the mind is silent.

Have you not noticed that love is silence? It may be while holding the hand of another, or looking lovingly at a child, or taking in the beauty of an evening. Love has no past or future, and so it is with this extraordinary state of silence. And without this silence, which is complete emptiness, there is no creation. You may be very clever in your capacity, but where there is no creation, there is destruction, decay, and the mind withers away.

When the mind is empty, silent, when it is in a state of complete negation—which is not blankness, nor the opposite of being positive, but a totally different state in which all thought has ceased—only then is it possible for that which is unnameable to come into being.

Eddington, Pennsylvania,
12 June 1936

THE MECHANISTIC VIEW of life is that, as man is merely the product of environment and of various reactions, perceptible only to the senses, the environment and reactions should be controlled by a rationalized system that will allow the individual to function only within its frame. Please comprehend the full significance of this mechanistic view of life. It conceives no supreme, transcendental entity, nothing that has a continuity; this view of life admits no survival of any kind after death; life is but a brief span leading to annihilation. As man is nothing but the result of environmental reactions, concerned with the pursuit of his own egotistic security, he has helped to create a system of exploitation, cruelty, and war. So his activities must be shaped and guided by changing and controlling the environment.

Then there are those who accept the view that man is essentially divine, that his destiny is controlled and guided by some supreme intelligence. These assert that they are seeking God, perfection, liberation, happiness, a state of being in which all subjective conflict has ceased. Their belief in a supreme entity who is guiding man's destiny is based on faith. They will say this transcendental entity or supreme intelligence has created the world and that the 'I', the ego, the individual, is something permanent in itself and has an eternal quality.

Sometimes you think life is mechanical, and at other times when there is sorrow and confusion, you revert to faith, looking to a supreme being for guidance and help. You vacillate between the opposites, whereas only through comprehension of the illusion of the opposites can you free yourself from their limitations and encumbrances. You often imagine that you are free from them, but you can be radically free only when you fully comprehend the process of the building up of these limitations and of bringing them to an end. You cannot possibly have the comprehension of the real, of what is, as long as this beginningless process of ignorance is perpetuated. When this process, sustaining itself through its own volitional activities of craving, ceases, there is that which may be called reality, truth, bliss.

From Talks in Europe 1967, *London, 30 September 1967*

PERHAPS IT WOULD be worthwhile to spend some time in trying to find out if life has any significance at all. Not the life that one leads, because modern existence has very little meaning. One gives intellectual significance to life, a theoretical, intellectual, theological, or (if one may use that word) mystical meaning to it; one tries to search out a deep meaning—as some writers have done amidst the despair of this hopeless existence—inventing some vital, deep, intellectual reason. And it seems to me that it would be very much worthwhile if we could find out for ourselves, not emotionally or intellectually, but actually, factually, if there is in life anything really sacred. Not the inventions of the mind that have given a sense of holiness to life, but actually whether there is such a thing. Because one observes both historically and actually in this search, in the life that one leads—the business, the competition, the despair, the loneliness, the anxiety, with the destruction of war and hate— life as all this has very little meaning. We may live seventy years, spending forty or fifty years in an office, with the routine, the boredom, and the loneliness of it that has very little meaning. Realizing that, both in the Orient and here, one then gives significance and worthwhileness to a symbol, to an idea, to a God— which are obviously the inventions of the mind. They have said in the East that life is one: don't kill; God exists in every human being: don't destroy. But the next minute they are destroying each other, actually, verbally, or in business, and so this idea that life is one, the sacredness of life, has very little meaning.

Also in the Occident, realizing what life actually is—the brutality, the aggressiveness, the ruthless competition of everyday life—one gives significance to a symbol. Those symbols upon which all religions are based are considered very holy. That is, the theologians, the priests, the saints who have had their peculiar experiences, have given meanings to life and we cling to those meanings out of our despair, out of our loneliness, out of our daily routine, which has so little meaning. And if we could put aside all the symbols, all the images, the ideas, and the beliefs that one has built throughout the centuries and to which one has given a sense of sacredness, if we could actually de-condition ourselves from all those extraneous inventions, then perhaps we could really ask ourselves if there is a something that is true, that is really holy and sacred. Because that is what man has been seeking amongst all this turmoil, despair, guilt, and death. Man has always sought in various forms this feeling of something that must be beyond the transitory, beyond the flux of time. Could we spend some time going into this and trying to find out for ourselves if there is such a thing?—but not what you want, not God, not an idea, not a symbol. Can one really brush all that aside and then find out?

Words are only a means of communication but the word is not the thing. The word, the symbol is not the actuality, and when one is caught up in words, then it becomes very difficult to extricate oneself from the symbols, the words, the ideas that actually prevent perception. Though one must use words, words are not the fact. So if we can also be aware, on guard, that the word is not the fact, then we can begin to go into this question very deeply. That is, man out of his loneliness and despair has given sacredness to an idea, to an image made by the hand or by the mind. The image has become extraordinarily important to the Christian, to the Hindu, to the Buddhist, and so on, and they have invested the sense of sacredness in that image. Can we brush it aside—not verbally, not theoretically, but actually push it aside—completely see the futility of such an activity? Then we can begin to ask. But there is no one to answer, because any fundamental question that we put to ourselves cannot be answered at all by anyone and least of all by ourselves. But what we can do is to put the question and let the question simmer, boil—let that question move. And one must have the capacity to follow that question right through. That is what we are asking: whether there is, beyond the symbol, the word, anything real, true, something completely holy in itself.

Seattle, 16 July 1950

Questioner: There are many concepts of God in the world today. What is your thought concerning God?

Krishnamurti: First of all, we must find out what we mean by a concept. What do we mean by the process of thinking? Because, after all, when we formulate a concept, let us say of God, our formula or concept must be the result of our conditioning, must it not? If we believe in God, surely our belief is the result of our environment. There are those who are trained from childhood to deny God and those who are trained to believe in God, as most of you have been. So we formulate a concept of God according to our training, according to our background, according to our idiosyncrasies, likes and dislikes, hopes and fears. Obviously then, as long as we do not understand the process of our own thinking, mere concepts of God have no value at all, have they? Because thought can project anything it likes. It can create and deny God. Each person can invent or destroy God according to his inclinations, pleasures, and pains. Therefore, as long as thought is active, formulating, inventing, that which is beyond time can never be discovered. God, or reality, is to be discovered only when thought comes to an end.

Now, when you ask, 'What is your thought concerning God?' you have already formulated your own thought, have you not? Thought can create God and experience that which it has created. But surely that is not true experience. It is only its own projection that thought experiences, and therefore it is not real. But if you and I can see the truth of this, then perhaps we shall experience something much greater than a mere projection of thought.

At the present time, when there is greater and greater insecurity outwardly, there is obviously a yearning for inward security. Since we cannot find security outside, we seek it in an idea, in thought, and so we create that which we call God, and that concept becomes our security. Now a mind that seeks security surely cannot find the real, the true. To understand that which is beyond time, the fabrications of thought must come to an end. Thought cannot exist without words, symbols, images. And only when the mind is quiet, free of its own creations, is there a possibility of finding out what is real. So merely to ask if there is or is not God is an immature response to the problem, is it not? To formulate opinions about God is really childish.

To experience, to realize that which is beyond time, we must obviously understand the process of time. The mind is the result of time, it is based on the memories of yesterday. And is it possible to be free from the multiplication of yesterdays that is the process of time? Surely this is a very serious problem; it is not a matter of belief or disbelief. Believing and disbelieving is a process of ignorance, whereas understanding the time-binding quality of thought brings freedom in which alone there can be discovery. But most of us want to believe because it is much more convenient; it gives us a sense of security, a sense of belonging to the group. Surely this very belief separates us; you believe in one thing and I believe in another. So belief acts as a barrier; it is a process of disintegration.

What is important, then, is not the cultivation of belief or disbelief, but to understand the process of the mind. It is the mind, it is thought that creates time. Thought is time, and whatever thought projects must be of time; therefore, thought cannot possibly go beyond itself. To discover what is beyond time, thought must come to an end, and that is a most difficult thing because the ending of thought does not come about through discipline, through control, through denial or suppression. Thought ends only when we understand the whole process of thinking, and to understand thinking there must be self-knowledge. Thought is the self, thought is the word that identifies itself as the 'me' and, at whatever level the self is placed, high or low, it is still within the field of thought.

To find God, that which is beyond time, we must understand the process of thought—that is, the process of oneself. The self is very complex; it is not at any one level, but is made up of many thoughts, many entities, each in contradiction with the others. There must be a constant awareness of them all, an awareness in which there is no choice, no condemnation or comparison; that is, there must be the capacity to see things as they are without distorting or translating them. The moment we judge or translate what is seen, we distort it according to our background. To discover reality or God, there can be no belief because acceptance or denial is a barrier to discovery. We all want to be secure both outwardly and inwardly, and the mind must understand that the search for security is an illusion. It is only the mind that is insecure, completely free from any form of possession that can discover—and this is an arduous task. It does not mean retiring into the woods, or to a monastery, or isolating oneself in some peculiar belief; on the contrary, nothing can exist in isolation. To be is to be related; it is only in the midst of relationship that we can spontaneously discover ourselves as we are. It is this very discovery of ourselves as we are, without any sense of condemnation or justification, that brings about a fundamental transformation in what we are. And that is the beginning of wisdom.

From Talks in Europe 1967, *Paris, 30 April 1967*

THE RELIGIOUS MIND is entirely different from the mind that believes in religion. The religious mind is psychologically free from the culture of society; it is also free from any form of belief, any form of demand for experience or self-expression. And man throughout the ages has created through belief a concept that is called God. To man the belief in the concept called God has been necessary because he finds life a sorrowful affair, an affair of constant battles, conflict, misery, with an occasional spark of light, beauty, and joy.

Belief in a concept, in a formula, in an idea, has become necessary because life has very little significance. The everyday routine, going to the office, the family, sex, the loneliness, the burden, the conflict of self-expression, all these have very little meaning— and there is always death at the end of it all. So man has to believe as an imperative necessity.

According to the climate, to the intellectual capacity of the inventors of these ideas and formulas, the concept of the God, the Saviour, the Master, took shape, and man has always been trying to reach thereby a state of bliss, of truth, the reality of a state of mind that must never be disturbed. So he has posited an end and worked towards it. The authors of these ideas and concepts have laid down either a system or a path that must be followed in order to achieve that ultimate reality. And man has tortured his mind— through discipline, through control, through self-denial, through abstinence, austerity—inventing different ways of approach to that reality. In Asia, there are many ways leading to that reality (at least they are said to) depending on temperament and circumstances, and those paths are followed to that reality that cannot be measured by man, by thought. In the Occident, there is only one Saviour; through Him alone is to be found that ultimate something. All the systems of the East and of the West imply constant control, constant twisting of the mind to conform to a pattern laid down by the priest, by the sacred books, by all those unfortunate things that are of the very essence of violence. Their violence is not only in the denying of the flesh, but also in the denial of every form of desire, every form of beauty, and in controlling and conforming to a certain pattern laid down.

They have had some kind of miracles—but miracles are the easiest of things to achieve, whether in the West or in the East. And those who achieve these miracles are anointed as saints; they have broken the record in that they have so completely conformed to the pattern that is expressed in their daily lives. They have very little humility, for humility cannot be shown outwardly—the putting on of a loincloth or rough robe is not an indication of humility at all. Like any virtue, humility is from moment to moment; it cannot be calculated, established, and laid down as a pattern to be followed. But man, throughout the ages, has done this; the originator, the original person who experienced something called reality, has laid down a system, a method, a way—and the rest of the world has followed. Then the disciples, through cunning propaganda, through cunning ways of capturing the mind of man, establish a church and dogmas, rituals. And man is caught in that—that any man who wishes to find that which mind is always seeking must go through some kind of twisting, some kind of suppression, some kind of torture, to come upon that ultimate beauty.

And so, intellectually, one sees the absurdity of all this; intellectually, verbally, one sees the absurdity of having any belief at all; one sees the idiocy of any ideology. Intellectually the mind may say it is nonsense and discard it, but inwardly there is always, deep down, the seeking beyond the rituals, beyond the dogmas, the beliefs, beyond the Saviours, beyond all the systems that are so obviously the invention of man. One sees that his Saviours, his Gods, are inventions, and one can discard these comparatively easily—and modern man is doing so. (I don't know why one uses the word *modern*—man has existed much as he is now for generations upon generations. But the present-day climate is such that he is denying totally the authority of priest, belief, and dogma, at the very root concept; to him, God is dead, and he died very young.) And as there is neither God nor belief, there is no concept other than of actual physical enjoyment, and physical satisfaction, and developing society: Man lives for the present, denying the whole of religious conception.

One begins by denying the outward gods, with their priests—of any organized religion—one must completely deny these because they have no value at all. They have bred wars, have separated men; whether in the Jewish religion, the Hindu religion, the Christian religion, or Islam—they have destroyed man, they have separated man, they have been one of the major causes of war, of violence. Seeing all this, one denies it, one puts it aside as something childish and immature. Intellectually one can do this very easily. Living in this world, observing the exploiting methods of the churches, temples, who can but deny? But it is much more difficult to be free of belief and of seeking at the psychological level. We all want to find something that is untouched by man, untouched by cunning thought, something that is not contaminated by any social, intellectual, or cultural society, something that cannot be destroyed by reason. We all seek it deeply, for this life is a travail, a battle, a misery, a routine. One may have the capacity to express oneself verbally, or in painting, in sculpture, in music, but even that becomes rather empty. Life as it is now is very empty and we try to fill it with music and literature, with amusement, with entertainment, with ideas, with knowledge; but when one goes into it a very little more deeply and widely, one discovers how empty one is, how shallow the whole of existence is—though one may have titles, possessions, capacities.

Life is empty, and realizing that we want to fill it. We are seeking, seeking ways and means, not only to fill this emptiness but also to find something that is not to be measured by man. Some may take drugs—LSD or another of the diverse forms of psychedelic drugs that give "expansion of consciousness"—and in that state one acquires or experiences certain results, because a certain sensitivity has been given to the brain. But these are chemical results. They are the results of extraneous outside agents. One takes drugs hopefully, then inwardly one has these experiences; as one has certain beliefs, so one experiences according to those beliefs; the processes are similar. Both produce an experience, yet man again gets lost in belief—in the drug of belief itself, or in the belief in the chemical drug. He is inevitably caught in his thoughts. And one sees through all that and discards it; that is, one is completely free of any belief. That does not mean that one becomes agnostic, or that one becomes cynical or bitter. On the contrary, you see the nature of belief and why belief becomes so extraordinarily important; it is because we are afraid—basically that is the reason. Because of fear—not only in the daily grind of life, the fear of not becoming, of not achieving psychically, not having power, position, prestige, fame—all this causes a great deal of fear and one puts up with that fear, but also because of this inward fear belief has become so important. Faced with the complete emptiness of life, one still holds on to belief; though one may discard the outward authority of belief—the belief invented by the priests throughout the world—one creates for oneself one's own belief in order to find and to come upon that extraordinary thing for which man has been searching, searching, searching.

And so one seeks. The nature, the structure, of search is very clear. Why does one seek at all? It is essentially self-interest—enlightened self-interest, but it is still self-interest. For one says: 'Life is so tawdry, empty, dull, stupid, there must be something more; I will go to that temple, to that church, to that. . . .' And then one discards all that, and one begins to seek deeply. But seeking, in any form, becomes a psychological hindrance. I think that must be understood very simply and clearly. One may objectively discard the authority of any outward agency that claims to lead to the ultimate truth, and that one does. But to discard because one understands the nature of searching, to discard all seekings, is necessary; because, one asks: 'What is one seeking?' If you examine what it is we are groping after, what it is that we want, is there not the implication of seeking something that you already know, that you have already lost, and you are trying to get at it? That is one of the implications of seeking. In seeking, there is involved the process of recognition—that is to say, when you find it, whatever it is, you must be able to recognize it—otherwise seeking has no meaning. Do, please, follow this. One seeks something hoping to find, and on finding it, to recognize it; but recognition is the action of memory; therefore there is the implication that you have already known it, that you have already had a glimpse. Or, as you are so heavily conditioned by the intense propaganda of all the organized religions, you mesmerize yourself into a state. So when you are seeking, you already have a concept, an idea of what you are seeking, and when you find it, it means that you already know it, otherwise you can't recognize it. For this reason it is not true at all.

Therefore one needs to find that state of mind that is really free from all search, from all belief—without becoming cynical, without stagnating. For we tend to think that if we do not seek, strive, struggle, grope after—endlessly—we shall wither away. And I don't know why we should not wither away—as though we are not withering away now. One does wither away; as one dies, as one grows older, the physical organism comes to an end. One's life is the process of withering, because in it, in daily life, we imitate, copy, follow, obey, conform—which are forms of withering. So a mind that is no longer caught in any form of belief, not caught in self-created belief, not seeking anything—though that may be a little more arduous—is tremendously alive. Truth is something that is only from moment to moment. Like virtue, like beauty, it is something that has no continuity. That which has continuity is the product of time, and time is thought.

Seeing what man has done to himself, how he has tortured himself, brutalized himself—becoming nationalistic, getting lost in some form of entertainment, whether it is literature, or this or that—seeing all this pattern of his life, one asks oneself, must one go through all this? Do you understand the question? Must a human being go through all this process, step by step—discarding belief (if you are at all alert), discarding any form of search, discarding the torturing of the mind, discarding indulgence? Seeing what man has done to himself in order to find what he calls reality, one asks—please ask yourself and not me—is there a way, or is there a state of explosion that discards it all at one breath? Because time is not the way.

Search implies time—taking perhaps ten years or more, or eventually finding through reincarnation as the whole of Asia believes. All this implies time—the gradual throwing away of these conflicts, these problems, becoming more wise, more cunning, getting to know slowly—gradually unconditioning the mind. Time implies that. Obviously time is not the way, nor belief, nor the artificial disciplines imposed by a system, by a guru, by a teacher, by a philosopher, by a priest—all that is so childish. So is it possible not to go through all this at all and yet come upon that extraordinary thing?—because that thing cannot be invited. Please do understand this very simple fact; it cannot be invited, it cannot be sought after; because the mind is too stupid, too small, our emotions are too shoddy, our ways of life are too confused for that enormity, for that immense something to be invited into that little house, into a petty though tidy room. One cannot invite it. To invite it, you must know it, and you cannot know it (it does not matter who says so) because the moment you say 'I know', you don't know. The moment you say you have found it, you have not found it. If you say you have experienced it, you have never experienced it. Those are all cunning ways of exploiting another man—the other man is your friend or your enemy.

Seeing all this—not formally, but in daily life, in your daily activities, when you pick up the pen, when you talk, when you go out for a drive or when you are walking alone in the woods—seeing all this at one glance—you don't have to read volumes to find it out—seeing all this with one breath, with one look, you can understand the whole thing. And you can only really understand this as a whole when you know yourself, know yourself as you are, very simply, as the result of the whole of mankind, whether you are a Hindu, a Moslem, a Christian, or whatever you are. There it is. When you know yourself as you are, then you understand the whole structure of man's endeavour, his deceptions, his hypocrisies, his brutality, his search.

And one asks if it is possible to come upon this thing without inviting, without waiting, without seeking, exploring, for that just to be, for it just to happen. Like a cool breeze that comes when you leave the window open—you cannot invite that breeze, but you must leave the window open. This does not mean that we are in a state of waiting—that is another form of deception; it does not mean that one must open oneself to receive—that again is another way of thought.

But if one has asked oneself without seeking, without believing, then in that very asking is the finding. But we do not ask. We want to be told, we want to have everything corroborated, affirmed; fundamentally, deep down, we are never free from every form of outward or inward authority. That is one of the most curious things in the structure of our psyche; we all want to be told; we are the result of what we have been told. What we have been told is the propaganda of thousands of years. There is the authority of the ancient book, of the present leader, or of the speaker. But if really deep down one denies all authority, it means one has no fears. To have no fear is to look at fear; but as with pleasure, we never come directly into contact with fear. We never actually come into contact with fear as you come in contact when touching a door, a hand, a face, a tree; we only come into contact with fear through the image of fear that we have created for ourselves. We only know pleasure through half-pleasures. We are never directly in contact with anything. I do not know if you have observed when you touch a tree—as you do when you are walking in the woods—if you are really touching the tree. Or is there a screen between you and the tree, although you are touching it? In the same way, in order to come directly into contact with fear there must be no image, which means actually having no memory of yesterday's fear. Then only do you come into actual contact with the actual fear of today. Then, if there is no memory of the fear of yesterday, you have the energy to meet the immediate fear, and you have to have a tremendous energy to meet the present. We dissipate this vital energy—that all of us have—through this image, through this formula, through this authority; and it is the same in the seeking of pleasure. The pursuit of pleasure is very important to us. The greatest pleasure of all is God—supposed to be—and that may be the most frightening thing you could ever know—but we have imagined it, the ultimate, so we never come upon it. Again, it is as when you have already recognized a pleasure as a pleasure of yesterday; you are really never in contact with actual experience, with an actual state. It is always the memory of yesterday that covers and screens the present.

So, seeing all this, is it possible not to do a thing, not strive, not seek, to be totally negative, totally empty, without any action? Because all action is the result of ideation. If you have observed yourself acting, you will have seen that it takes place because of a previous idea, a previous concept, a previous memory. There is a division between the idea and the action, an interval however small, however minute, and because of that division there is conflict. Can the mind be so completely quiet, neither thinking nor afraid, and therefore extraordinarily alive, intense?

You know the word *passion;* that word so often signifies suffering; the Christians have used that word to symbolize certain forms of suffering. We are not using the word *passion* in that sense at all. In this complete state of negation is the highest form of passion. That passion implies total self-abandonment. For such complete self-abandonment there must be tremendous austerity, austerity that is not the harshness of the priest agonizing people, of saints who have tortured themselves, who have become austere because they have brutalized their minds. Austerity is really an extraordinary simplicity, not in clothes, not in food, but inwardly. This austerity, this passion, is the highest form of total negation. And then perhaps, if you are lucky—there is no luck there, the thing comes uninvited—then the mind is no longer capable of striving. Then you do what you will, because then there will be love.

Without this religious mind, a true society cannot be created. We must create a new society in which this terrible activity of self-interest has very little place. It is only with such a religious mind that there can be peace, outwardly as well as inwardly.

From The First and Last Freedom, *Chapter 28*

Questioner: Our mind knows only the known. What is it in us that drives us to find the unknown, reality, God?

Krishnamurti: Does your mind urge towards the unknown? Is there an urge in us for the unknown, for reality, for God? Please think it out seriously. This is not a rhetorical question; let us actually find out. Is there an inward urge in each one of us to find the unknown? Is there? How can you find the unknown? If you do not know it, how can you find it? Is there an urge for reality, or is it merely a desire for the known expanded? Do you understand what I mean? I have known many things; they have not given me happiness, satisfaction, joy. So now I am wanting something else that will give me greater joy, greater happiness, greater vitality—what you will. Can the known, which is my mind—because my mind is the known, the result of the past—can that mind seek the unknown? If I do not know reality, the unknown, how can I search for it? Surely it must come, I cannot go after it. If I go after it, I am going after something that is the known, projected by me.

Our problem is not what it is in us that drives us to find the unknown. That is clear enough; it is our own desire to be more secure, more permanent, more established, more happy; to escape from turmoil, from pain, confusion. That is our obvious drive. When there is that drive, that urge, you will find a marvellous escape, a marvellous refuge—in the Buddha, in the Christ, or in political slo-gans and all the rest of it. That is not reality; that is not the un-knowable, the unknown. Therefore the urge for the unknown must come to an end, the search for the unknown must stop, which means there must be understanding of the cumulative known, which is the mind. The mind must understand itself as the known, because that is all it knows. You cannot think about something that you do not know. You can only think about something that you know.

Our difficulty is for the mind not to proceed in the known; that can only happen when the mind understands itself and how all its movement is from the past, projecting itself through the present to the future. It is one continuous movement of the known. Can that movement come to an end? It can come to an end only when the mechanism of its own process is understood, only when the mind understands itself and its workings, its ways, its purposes, its pur-suits, its demands—not only the superficial demands but the deep inward urges and motives. This is quite an arduous task. It isn't just in a meeting or at a lecture or by reading a book that you are going to find out. On the contrary, it needs constant watchfulness, constant awareness of every movement of thought, not only when you are awake, but also when you are asleep. It must be a total process, not a sporadic, partial process.

Also, the intention must be right. That is, there must be a cessation of the superstition that inwardly we all want the unknown. It is an illusion to think that we are all seeking God; we are not. We don't have to search for light. There will be light when there is no darkness, and through darkness we cannot find the light. All that we can do is to remove those barriers that create darkness, and the re-moval depends on the intention. If you are removing them in order to see light, then you are not removing anything, you are only sub-stituting the word *light* for darkness. Even to look beyond the dark-ness is an escape from darkness.

We have to consider not what it is that is driving us, but why there is in us such confusion, such turmoil, such strife and an-tagonism—all the stupid things of our existence. When these are not, then there is light, we don't have to look for it. When stupidity is gone, there is intelligence. But the man who is stupid and tries to become intelligent is still stupid. Stupidity can never be made wisdom; only when stupidity ceases is there wisdom, intelligence. The man who is stupid and tries to become intelligent, wise, obviously can never be so. To know what is stupidity, one must go into it, not superficially, but fully, completely, deeply, profoundly; one must go into all the different layers of stupidity, and when there is the cessation of that stupidity, there is wisdom.

Therefore it is important to find out not if there is something more, something greater than the known, which is urging us to the unknown, but to see what it is in us that is creating confusion, wars, class differences, snobbishness, the pursuit of the famous, the accumulation of knowledge, the escape through music, through art, through so many ways. It is important, surely, to see them as they are and to come back to ourselves as we are. From there we can proceed. Then the throwing off of the known is comparatively easy. When the mind is silent, when it is no longer projecting itself into the future, wishing for something, when the mind is really quiet, profoundly peaceful, the unknown comes into being. You don't have to search for it. You cannot invite it. That which you can invite is only that which you know. You cannot invite an unknown guest. You can only invite one you know. But you do not know the unknown, God, reality, or what you will. It must come. It can come only when the field is right, when the soil is tilled, but if you till in order for it to come, then you will not have it.

Our problem is not how to seek the unknowable, but to understand the accumulative processes of the mind that is ever the known. That is an arduous task; that demands constant attention, a constant awareness in which there is no sense of distraction, of identification, of condemnation; it is being with what is. Then only can the mind be still. No amount of meditation, discipline, can make the mind still—in the real sense of the word. Only when the breezes stop does the lake become quiet. You cannot make the lake quiet. Our job is not to pursue the unknowable, but to understand the confusion, the turmoil, the misery, in ourselves. And then that thing darkly comes into being in which there is joy.

From Life Ahead, *Chapter 4*

Questioner: What is God?

Krishnamurti: How are you going to find out? Are you going to accept somebody else's information? Or are you going to try to discover for yourself what God is? It is easy to ask questions, but to experience the truth requires a great deal of intelligence, a great deal of inquiry and search.

So the first question is: Are you going to accept what another says about God? It does not matter who it is, Krishna, Buddha, or Christ, because they may all be mistaken—and so may your own particular guru be mistaken. Surely, to find out what is true, your mind must be free to inquire, which means that it cannot merely accept or believe. I can give you a description of the truth, but it will not be the same thing as your experiencing the truth for yourself. All the sacred books describe what God is, but those descriptions are not God. The word *God* is not God, is it?

To find out what is true you must never accept, you must never be influenced by what the books, the teachers, or anyone else may say. If you are influenced by them, you will find only what they want you to find. And you must know that your own mind can create the image of what it wants; it can imagine God with a beard, or with one eye; it can make Him blue or purple. So you have to be aware of your own desires and not be deceived by the projections of your own wants and longings. If you long to see God in a certain form, the image you see will be according to your wishes, and that image will not be God, will it? If you are in sorrow and want to be comforted, or if you feel sentimental and romantic in your religious aspirations, eventually you will create a God who will supply what you want, but it will still not be God.

So your mind must be completely free, and only then can you find out what is true—not by the acceptance of some superstition, nor by the reading of the so-called sacred books, nor by following some guru. Only when you have this freedom, this real freedom from external influences as well as from your own desires and longings so that your mind is very clear—only then is it possible to find out what God is. But if you merely sit down and speculate, then your guess is as good as your guru's, and equally illusory.

Q: Can we be aware of our unconscious desires?

K: First of all, are you aware of your conscious desires? Do you know what desire is? Are you aware that usually you do not listen to anyone who is saying something contrary to what you believe? Your desire prevents you from listening. If you desire God, and somebody points out that the God you desire is the outcome of your frustrations and fears, will you listen to him? Of course not. You want one thing, and the truth is something quite different. You limit yourself within your own desires. You are only half aware of your conscious desires, are you not? And to be aware of the desires that are deeply hidden is much more difficult. To find out what is hidden, to discover what its own motives are, the mind that is seeking must be fairly clear and free. So first be fully aware of your conscious desires; then, as you become increasingly aware of what is on the surface, you can go deeper and deeper.

From Life Ahead, *Chapter 7, with Young People*

Questioner: What is the easiest way of finding God?

Krishnamurti: I am afraid there is no easy way, because to find God is a most difficult, a most arduous thing. Is not what we call God something that the mind creates? You know what the mind is. The mind is the result of time, and it can create anything, any illusion. It has the power of creating ideas, of projecting itself in fancies, in imagination; it is constantly accumulating, discarding, choosing. Being prejudiced, narrow, limited, the mind can picture God, it can imagine what God is according to its own limitations. Because certain teachers, priests, and so-called saviours have said there is God and have described him, the mind can imagine God in those terms, but that image is not God. God is something that cannot be found by the mind.

To understand God, you must first understand your own mind. That is very difficult. The mind is very complex, and to understand it is not easy. But it is easy enough to sit down and go into some kind of dream, have various visions, illusions, and then think that you are very near to God. The mind can deceive itself enormously. So to really experience that which may be called God, you must be completely quiet—and have you not found out how extremely difficult that is? Have you not noticed how even the older people never sit quietly, how they fidget, how they wiggle their toes and move their hands? It is difficult physically to sit still, and how much more difficult it is for the mind to be still! You may follow some guru and force your mind to be quiet; but your mind is not really quiet. It is still restless, like a child that is made to stand in the corner. It is a great art for the mind to be completely silent without coercion, and only then is there a possibility of experiencing that which may be called God.

Q: Is God everywhere?

K: Are you really interested to find out? You ask questions, and then subside; you do not listen. Have you noticed how the older people almost never listen to you? They rarely listen to you because they are so enclosed in their own thoughts, in their own emotions, in their own satisfactions and sorrows. I hope you have noticed this. If you know how to observe and how to listen, really listen, you will find out a lot of things, not only about people but about the world.

Here is this boy asking if God is everywhere. He is rather young to be asking that question. He does not know what it really means. He probably has a vague inkling of something—the feeling of beauty, an awareness of the birds in the sky, of running waters, of a nice, smiling face, of a leaf dancing in the wind, of a woman carrying a burden. And there is anger, noise, sorrow—all that is in the air. So he is naturally interested and anxious to find out what life is all about. He hears the older people talking about God, and he is puzzled. It is very important for him to ask such a question, is it not? And it is equally important for you all to seek the answer; because, as I said the other day, you will begin to catch the meaning of all this inwardly, unconsciously, deep down; and then, as you grow up, you will have hints of other things besides this ugly world of struggle. The world is beautiful, the earth is bountiful, but we are the spoilers of it.

Q: What is the real goal of life?

K: It is, first of all, what you make of it. It is what you make of life.

Q: As far as reality is concerned, it must be something else. I am not particularly interested in having a personal goal, but I want to know what is the goal for everybody.

K: How will you find out? Who will show you? Can you discover that by reading? If you read, one author may give you a particular method, while another author may offer quite a different method. If you go to a man who is suffering, he will say that the goal of life is to be happy. If you go to a man who is starving, who has not had sufficient food for years, his goal will be to have a full tummy. If you go to a politician, his goal will be to become one of the directors, one of the rulers of the world. If you ask a young woman, she will say, 'My goal is to have a baby.' If you go to a sannyasi, his goal is to find God. The goal, the underlying desire of people is generally to find something gratifying, comforting; they want some form of security, safety, so that they will have no doubts, no questions, no anxiety, no fear. Most of us want something permanent to which we can cling, do we not?

So the general goal of life for man is some kind of hope, some kind of safety, some kind of permanency. Don't say, 'Is that all?' That is the immediate fact, and you must first be fully acquainted with that. You must question all that—which means, you must question yourself. The general goal of life for man is embedded in you, because you are part of the whole. You yourself want safety, permanency, happiness; you want something to which to cling.

Now to find out if there is something else beyond, some truth that is not of the mind, all the illusions of the mind must be finished with; that is, you must understand them and put them aside. Only then can you discover the real thing, whether there is a goal or not. To stipulate that there must be a goal, or to believe that there is a goal, is merely another illusion. But if you can question all your conflicts, struggles, pains, vanities, ambitions, hopes, fears, and go through them, go beyond and above them, then you will find out.

Q: If I develop higher influences will I eventually see the ultimate?

K: How can you see the ultimate as long as there are many barriers between you and that? First you must remove the barriers. You cannot sit in a closed room and know what fresh air is like. To have fresh air you must open the windows. Similarly, you must see all the barriers, all the limitations and conditionings within yourself; you must understand them and put them aside. Then you will find out. But to sit on this side and try to find out what is on the other has no meaning.

From Commentaries on Living
First Series, *Chapter 18*

THE LONG EVENING shadows were over the still waters, and the
river was becoming quiet after the day. Fish were jumping out of the
water, and the heavy birds were coming to roost among the big trees.
There was not a cloud in the sky, which was silver-blue. A boat full
of people came down the river; they were singing and clapping, and
a cow called in the distance. There was the scent of evening. A garland of marigold was moving with the water that sparkled in the
setting sun. How beautiful and alive it all was—the river, the birds,
the trees, and the villagers.

> We were sitting under a tree, overlooking the river. Near
the tree was a small temple, and a few lean cows wandered about.
The temple was clean and well swept, and the flowering bush was
watered and cared for. A man was performing his evening rituals,
and his voice was patient and sorrowful. Under the last rays of the
sun, the water was the colour of newborn flowers. Presently someone joined us and began to talk of his experiences. He said he had
devoted many years of his life to the search for God, had practised
many austerities and renounced many things that were dear. He had
also helped considerably in social work, in building a school, and so
on. He was interested in many things, but his consuming interest
was the finding of God, and now, after many years, His voice was
being heard, and it guided him in little as well as big things. He

had no will of his own, but followed the inner voice of God. It never failed him, though he often corrupted its clarity; his prayer was ever for the purification of the vessel, that it might be worthy to receive.

Can that which is immeasurable be found by you and me? Can that which is not of time be searched out by that thing which is fashioned of time? Can a diligently practised discipline lead us to the unknown? Is there a means to that which has no beginning and no end? Can that reality be caught in the net of our desires? What we can capture is the projection of the known; but the unknown cannot be captured by the known. That which is named is not the unnameable, and by naming we only awaken the conditioned responses. These responses, however noble and pleasant, are not of the real. We respond to stimulants, but reality offers no stimulant: It is.

The mind moves from the known to the known, and it cannot reach out into the unknown. You cannot think of something you do not know; it is impossible. What you think about comes out of the known, the past, whether that past be remote, or the second that has just gone by. This past is thought, shaped and conditioned by many influences, modifying itself according to circumstances and pressures, but ever remaining a process of time. Thought can only deny or assert, it cannot discover or search out the new. Thought cannot come upon the new, but when thought is silent, then there may be the new—which is immediately transformed into the old, into the experienced, by thought. Thought is ever shaping, modifying, colouring according to a pattern of experience. The function of thought is to communicate but not to be in the state of experiencing. When experiencing ceases, then thought takes over and terms it within the category of the known. Thought cannot penetrate into the unknown, and so it can never discover or experience reality.

Disciplines, renunciations, detachment, rituals, the practice of virtue—all these, however noble, are the process of thought; and thought can only work towards an end, towards an achievement, which is ever the known. Achievement is security, the self-protective certainty of the known. To seek security in that which is nameless is to deny it. The security that may be found is only in the projection of the past, of the known. For this reason the mind must be entirely and deeply silent; but this silence cannot be purchased through sacrifice, sublimation, or suppression. This silence comes when the mind is no longer seeking, no longer caught in the process of becoming. This silence is not cumulative, it may not be built up through practice. The silence must be as unknown to the mind as the timeless; for if the mind experiences the silence, then there is the experiencer who is the result of past experiences, who is cognizant of a past silence; and what is experienced by the experiencer is merely a self-projected repetition. The mind can never experience the new, and so the mind must be utterly still.

The mind can be still only when it is not experiencing, that is, when it is not terming or naming, recording or storing up in memory. This naming and recording is a constant process of the different layers of consciousness, not merely of the upper mind. But when the superficial mind is quiet, the deeper mind can offer up its intimations. When the whole consciousness is silent and tranquil, free from all becoming, which is spontaneity, then only does the immeasurable come into being. The desire to maintain this freedom gives continuity to the memory of the becomer, which is a hindrance to reality. Reality has no continuity; it is from moment to moment, ever new, ever fresh. What has continuity can never be creative.

The upper mind is only an instrument of communication, it cannot measure that which is immeasurable. Reality is not to be spoken of; when it is, it is no longer reality.

This is meditation.

Bombay, 3 March 1965

It seems to me that man for so many centuries has always sought peace, freedom, and a state of bliss that he calls God. He has sought it under different names and at different periods in history, and apparently only a very few have found that inward sense of great peace, freedom, and that state that man has called God. In modern times it has become of such little importance; we use the word *God* with very little meaning. We are always seeking a state of bliss, peace, and freedom away from this world, and we take flight in various forms from this world to find something that will be enduring, that will give us sanctuary and sanctity, that will give us a certain sense of deep inward quietness. Whether one believes in God or not depends on mental influence, tradition, climate. To find that state of bliss, that freedom, that extraordinary peace, it must be a living thing. One must understand, I think, why one is not capable of facing the fact and transforming the fact, and thereby going beyond it.

I would like, if I may, to talk about—or rather communicate together about—why we always give such great importance to idea and not to action. Though we have talked about it in different ways and at different times, I would like to go into it in a different way, because it seems to me that we are responsible totally, completely, for the society in which we live. For the misery, for the confusion, for the utter brutality of modern existence, each one of us is totally and completely responsible. We cannot possibly escape from it; we have to transform it. The human being who is part of society and has created this society—for this he is totally and completely responsible—must transform it, and to bring about a mutation, a transformation within himself and thereby within the pattern of society, is only possible when he ceases completely to escape into ideas.

God is an idea depending on the climate, the environment, and the tradition in which you have been brought up. In the Communist world, depending on those circumstances, people do not believe in God. Here you are dependent on your circumstances, on your life, and on your tradition, and you have built up your idea. One must liberate oneself from these circumstances, from society; and only then is it possible for a human being, in this freedom, to find that which is true. But merely to escape into an idea called *God* does not solve the problem at all.

'God'—or any other name you would like to use—is the cunning invention of man, and we cover that invention, that cunningness, by incense, by ritual, by various forms of belief, dogmas, separating man as Catholics, Hindus, Moslems, Parsis, Buddhists— all the clever cunning structure invented by man. Man, having invented it, is caught in it. Without understanding the present world, the world he lives in—the world of his misery, the world of his confusion, sorrow, anxiety, despair, and the agony of existence, the complete loneliness, the sense of utter futility of life—without understanding all that, the mere multiplication of ideas, however satisfactory, has no value at all.

It is very important to understand why we create or formulate an idea. Why does the mind formulate an idea at all? I mean by *formulating*, making a structure of philosophical or rational or humanistic or materialistic ideas. Idea is organized thought; in that organized thought, belief, idea, man lives. That is what we all do, whether we are religious or non-religious. I think it is important to find out why human beings throughout the ages have given such an extraordinary importance to ideas. Why do we formulate ideas at all?. . . . We form ideas, if one observes oneself, when there is inattention. When you are completely active, which demands total attention—which is action—in that there is no idea; you are acting.

Please, if I may suggest, just listen. Don't accept or deny; don't build defences to prevent listening, by having your own thoughts, beliefs, contradictions, and all that. But just listen. We are not trying to convince you of anything; we are not forcing you through any means to conform to a particular idea, or pattern, or action. We are merely stating facts—whether you like them or not—and what is important is to learn about the fact. 'Learning' implies total listening, a complete observation. When you listen to the sound of the crow [in the trees where he is speaking], do not listen with your own noises, with your own fears, thoughts, with your own ideas, with your own opinions. Then you will see that there is no idea at all, but you are actually listening.

In the same way, if I may suggest, just listen. Just listen, not only consciously but also unconsciously—which is perhaps much more important. Most of us are influenced. We can reject conscious influences; but it is much more difficult to put aside the unconscious influences. When you are listening in this manner, then it is neither conscious nor unconscious listening. Then you are completely attentive. And attention is not yours or mine; it is not nationalistic, it is not religious, it is not divisible. When you are so completely listening, there is no idea; there is only a state of listening. Most of us do this when we are listening to something rather beautiful, when there is lovely music, or when you are seeing a mountain, the light of the evening, or the light on the water, or a cloud. Then in that state of attention, in that state of listening, seeing, there is no idea.

In the same way if you could listen with that ease, with that effortless attention, then perhaps you will see the great significance of idea and action. Most of us formulate ideas when there is inattention. We create or conceive ideas when those ideas give us security, a sense of certainty. And that sense of certainty, that sense of being safe, brings about ideas, and into those ideas we escape; and therefore there is no action. We create or formulate ideas when we do not completely comprehend that which is. So ideas become much more important than the fact.

To find out—actually to find out the fact—if there is God, or if there is no God, ideas have no meaning whatsoever. Whether you believe or don't believe, whether you are a theist or an atheist, it has no meaning. To find out, you need all your energy, your complete, total energy, energy that is not spotted, that is not scratched, energy that has no twist, that has not been made corrupt.

So to understand, to find out if there is such a thing as that reality that man has sought for so many millions of years, one must have energy—energy that is completely whole, uncontaminated. And to bring about that energy, we must understand effort.

Most of us spend our life in effort, in struggle, and the effort, the struggle, the striving, is a dissipation of that energy. Man, throughout the historical period, has said that to find that reality or God—whatever name he may give to it—you must be a celibate; that is, you take a vow of chastity and suppress, control, battle with yourself endlessly all your life to keep your vow. Look at the waste of energy! It is also a waste of energy to indulge. And it has far more significance when you suppress. The effort that has gone into suppression, into control, into this denial of your desire, distorts your mind, and through that distortion you have a certain sense of austerity, which becomes harsh. Please listen. Observe it in yourself and observe the people around you. And observe this waste of energy, the battle—not the implications of sex, not the actual act, but the ideals, the images, the pleasure—the constant thought about them is a waste of energy. And most people waste their energy either through denial, or through a vow of chastity, or in thinking about it endlessly.

Man is responsible—you and I are responsible—for the condition of the society in which we live. You are responsible, not your politicians, because you have made the politicians what they are—crooked, glorifying themselves, seeking position and prestige—which is what we are doing in daily life. We are responsible for society. The psychological structure of society is far more important than the organizational side of society. The psychological structure of society is based on greed, envy, acquisitiveness, competition, ambition, fear, this incessant demand of a human being wanting to be secure in all his relationships, secure in property, secure in his relationship to people, secure in his relationship to ideas. That is the structure of society that one has created. And society then imposes the structure psychologically on each one of us. Greed, envy, ambition, competition, all that is a waste of energy, because in it there is always conflict—conflict that is endless, as in a person who is jealous.

Jealousy is an idea. The idea and the fact are two different things. Please listen. You approach the feeling called 'jealousy' through the idea. You do not come directly into contact with the feeling called jealousy. But you approach jealousy through the memory of a certain word that you have established in your mind as jealousy. It becomes an idea, and that idea prevents you from coming directly into contact with that feeling that you call jealousy. Again, this is a fact. So the formula, the idea, prevents you from coming directly into contact with that feeling, and therefore the idea dissipates this energy.

As *we* are responsible for the misery, for the poverty, for wars, for the utter lack of peace, a religious man does not seek God. The religious man is concerned with the transformation of society that is himself. The religious man is not the man that does innumerable rituals, follows traditions, lives in a dead, past culture, explaining endlessly the Gita or the Bible, endlessly chanting, or taking vows. That is not a religious man; such a man is escaping from facts. The religious man is concerned totally and completely with the understanding of society that is himself. He is not separate from society. Bringing about in himself a complete, total mutation means complete cessation of greed, envy, ambition; and therefore he is not dependent on circumstances, though he is the result of circumstances—the food he eats, the books he reads, the cinemas he goes to, the religious dogmas, beliefs, rituals, and all that business. He is responsible; and therefore the religious man must understand himself, who is the product of society that he himself has created. Therefore to find reality he must begin here, not in a temple, not in an image—whether the image is graven by the hand or by the mind. Otherwise how can he find something totally new, a new state?

Peace is not merely the expansion of law or sovereignty. Peace is something entirely different; it is an inward state that cannot possibly come by the alteration of outer circumstances, though the change of outer circumstances is necessary. But it must begin within to bring about a different world. And to bring about a different world you need tremendous energy, and that energy is now being dissipated in constant conflict. Therefore, one must understand this conflict.

The primary cause of conflict is escape—escape through idea. Please observe yourself: Instead of facing—let us say—jealousy, envy, instead of coming directly into contact with it, you say, 'How shall I get over it? What shall I do? What are the methods by which I cannot be jealous?'—which are all ideas and therefore an escape from the fact that you are jealous, a going away from the fact that you are jealous. The going away from the fact through ideas not only wastes your energy, but prevents you from coming into contact directly with that fact. You have to give your complete attention, not through an idea. Idea, as we pointed out, prevents attention. So when you observe, or become aware of, this feeling of jealousy, and give complete attention to it without ideas, then you will see that not only are you directly in contact with that feeling, but because you have given your complete attention, not through ideas, it ceases to be. You then have greater energy to meet the next incident, or the next emotion, the next feeling.

To discover, to bring about a complete mutation, you must have energy—not the energy that is brought about through suppression, but that energy that comes to you when you are not escaping through ideas or through suppression. Really, if you think of it, we know only two ways to meet life—either we escape from it altogether, which is a form of insanity leading to neurosis, or we suppress everything because we do not understand. That is all we know.

Suppression is not only putting the lid on any feeling or any sensation, but it is also a form of intellectual explanation, rationalization. Please observe yourself and you will see how factual is what is being said. So it is necessary that you do not escape. And it is one of the most important things to find out, never to escape. It is one of the most difficult things—to find out—because we escape through words. We escape from the fact not only by running to the temple and all the rest of that business, but through words, through intellectual arguments, opinions, judgments. We have so many ways of escaping from the fact. For example, take the fact that one is dull. If one is dull, that is a fact. And when you become conscious that you are dull, the escape is to try to become clever. But to become sensitive demands that all your attention be directed to that state of mind which is dull.

So we need energy, which is not the result of any contradiction, any tension, but which comes about when there is no effort at all. Please do understand this one very simple, actual fact: that we waste our energy through effort, and that waste of energy through effort prevents us from coming directly into contact with the fact. When I am making a tremendous effort to listen to you, all my energy is gone in making the effort, and I am not actually listening. When I am angry or impatient, all my energy is gone in trying to say, 'I must not be angry.' But when I pay attention completely to anger, or to that state of mind, by not escaping through words, through condemnation, through judgment, then in that state of attention there is a freedom from that thing called anger. Therefore that attention that is the summation of energy is not effort. It is only the mind that is without effort that is the religious mind. And, therefore, such a mind alone can find out if there is, or if there is not, God.

Then there is another factor: We are imitative human beings. There is nothing original. We are the result of time, of many,

many thousand yesterdays. From our childhood we have been brought up to imitate, to obey, to copy tradition, to follow the scriptures, to follow authority. We are not talking of the authority of law that must be obeyed, but we are talking of the authority of the scriptures, the spiritual authority, the pattern, the formula. We obey and imitate.

When you imitate—which is to conform inwardly to a pattern, whether imposed by society, or by yourself through your own experience—such conformity, such imitation, such obedience, destroys the clarity of energy. You imitate, you conform, you obey authority, because you are frightened. A man who understands, who sees clearly, who is very attentive, has no fear; therefore, he has no reason to imitate. He is himself—whatever that himself may be—at every moment.

So imitation, conformity to a religious pattern, or nonconformity to a religious pattern but conformity to one's own experience, is still the outcome of fear. And a man who is afraid—whether of God, whether of society, whether of himself—such a man is not a religious man. And a man is only free when there is no fear. Therefore, he must come into contact with fear directly, not through the idea of fear.

The coming together of that unspotted, uncorrupted, vital energy can only happen when you reject. I do not know if you have noticed that when you reject something not as a reaction, that very rejection creates energy. When you reject, let us say, ambition—not because you want to be spiritual, not because you want to live a peaceful life, not because you want God or anything else, but for itself—when you see the utter destructive nature of conflict involved in ambition and reject it, that very rejection is energy. I do not know if you have ever rejected anything. When you reject a particular pleasure—for instance, when you reject the pleasure of smoking, not because your doctor has told you that it is bad for your lungs, not because you have no money to smoke umpteen cigarettes a day, not because you are caught in a slavish habit, but because you see it has no meaning—when you reject it without a reaction, that very rejection brings an energy. Similarly, when you reject society—not run away from it as the sannyasi, the monk, and the so-called religious people do, when you reject the psychological structure of society totally—out of that rejection you have tremendous energy. The very act of rejection is energy.

Now you have seen for yourself, or understood, or have listened to, the nature of conflict, effort, which dissipates energy. And you have understood or realized, not verbally but actually, this sense of energy that is not the outcome of conflict, but which comes when the mind has understood the whole network of escapes, suppression, conflict, imitation, fear. Then you can proceed, then you can begin to find out for yourself what is real, not as an escape, not as a means of avoiding your responsibility in this world. You can only find out what is real, what is good—if there is good—not through belief, but through transforming yourself in your relationship with your property, with people, and with ideas, and therefore being free from society. Only then have you that energy to find out, not by escaping or suppressing.

If you have gone that far, then you must begin to find out the nature of the discipline, the austerity that one has, either traditionally, or because you have understood. There is a natural process of austerity, a natural process of discipline, which is not harsh, which does not conform, which is not merely imitating a particular pleasurable habit. And when you have done this, you will find there is an intelligence of the highest form of sensitivity. Without this sensitivity, you have no beauty.

A religious mind must be aware of this extraordinary sense of sensitivity and beauty. The religious mind of which we are talking is entirely different from the religious mind of the orthodox. Because to the religious mind of the orthodox there is no beauty; he is totally unaware of the world in which we live—the beauty of the world, the beauty of the earth, the beauty of the hill, the beauty of a tree, the beauty of a nice face with a smile on it. To him beauty is temptation; to him beauty is the woman, whom he must avoid at all costs to find God. Such a mind is not a religious mind, because it is not sensitive to the world—to the world of beauty, to the world of squalor. You cannot be sensitive only to beauty; you must also be sensitive to squalor, to dirt, to the disorganized human mind. Sensitivity means sensitivity all around, not just in one particular direction. So a mind that is not in itself aware of this beauty, cannot proceed further. There must be this quality of sensitivity.

Then such a mind, which is the religious mind, understands the nature of death. Because if it does not understand death, it does not understand love. Death is not the end of life. Death is not an event brought about by disease, by senility, by old age, or by accident. Death is something that you live every day with, because you are dying every day to everything that you know. If you do not know death, you will never know what love is.

Love is not memory; love is not a symbol, a picture, an idea; love is not a social act; love is not a virtue. If there is love, you are virtuous; you do not have to struggle to be virtuous. But there is no love, because you have never understood what it is to die—to die to your experience, to die to your pleasures, to die to your particular form of secret memory of which you are not aware. And when you bring out all that and die every minute—die to your house, to your memories, to your pleasures—voluntarily and easily and without effort, then you will know what love is.

And without beauty, without the sense of death, without love, you will never find reality; do what you will, go to all the temples, follow every guru invented by every unintelligent man, you will never find reality that way. Reality is creation.

Creation does not mean producing babies, or painting a picture, or writing a poem, or producing a good dish of food. That is not creation, that is merely the result of a particular talent, a gift, or learning a particular technique. An invention is not creation. Creation can come about only when you are dead to time; that is, when there is no tomorrow. Creation can only take place when there is complete concentration of energy that has no movement at all within or without.

Please follow this. Whether you understand it or not does not matter. Our life is so shoddy, so miserable; there is so much despair and so much misery. We have lived for two million years, and there is nothing new. We know only repetition, boredom, and the utter futility of every act that we do. To bring about a new mind, a sense of innocence, a sense of freshness, there must be this sensitivity, this death and love, and that creation. That creation can come about when there is this complete energy that has no movement in any direction.

Look! When the mind faces a problem, it is always seeking a way out by trying to solve it, to overcome it, to go round it or beyond it or above it, by always doing something with the problem, moving out or within. If it did not move in any direction—when there is no movement at all, within or without, but there is only the problem—then there would be an explosion in that problem. You do it sometime and you will see the actuality of what is being said— which you do not have to believe, to argue, or not to argue. There is no authority here.

So when there is this concentration of energy that is the outcome of no effort, and when that energy has no movement in any direction, at that moment there is creation. And that creation is truth, God, or what you will—word has no meaning then. Then that explosion, that creation, is peace; you do not have to seek peace. That creation is beauty. That creation is love.

It is only such a religious mind that can bring about order in this confused, sorrowing world. And it is your responsibility—yours and nobody else's—while living in this world, to bring about such a creative life. And it is only such a mind that is the religious mind and the blessed mind.

Bangalore, 4 July 1948

Questioner: Man must know what God is before he can know God. How are you going to introduce the idea of God to man without bringing God to man's level?

Krishnamurti: You cannot, sir. Now, what is the impetus behind the search for God, and is that search real? For most of us it is an escape from actuality. So we must be very clear in ourselves whether this search after God is an escape or whether it is a search for truth in everything—truth in our relationships, truth in the value of things, truth in ideas. If we are seeking God merely because we are tired of this world and its miseries, then it is an escape. Then we create God, and therefore it is not God. The God of the temples, of the books, is not God; obviously, it is a marvellous escape. But if we try to find the truth, not in one exclusive set of actions, but in all our actions, ideas, and relationships, if we seek the right evaluation of food, clothing, and shelter, then because our minds are capable of clarity and understanding, when we seek reality we shall find it. It will not then be an escape. But if we are confused with regard to the things of the world—food, clothing, shelter, relationship, and ideas—how can we find reality? We can only invent 'reality'. So, God, truth, or reality, is not to be known by a mind that is confused, conditioned, limited. How can such a mind think of reality or God?

It has first to de-condition itself. It has to free itself from its own limitations, and only then can it know what God is; obviously, not before. Reality is the unknown, and that which is known is not the real.

So, a mind that wishes to know reality has to free itself from its own conditioning, and that conditioning is imposed either externally or internally; and as long as the mind creates contention, conflict in relationship, it cannot know reality. So if one is to know reality, the mind must be tranquil; but if the mind is compelled, disciplined to be tranquil, that tranquillity is in itself a limitation, it is merely self-hypnosis. The mind becomes free and tranquil only when it understands the values with which it is surrounded. So to understand that which is the highest, the supreme, the real, we must begin very low, very near; that is, we have to find the value of things, of relationship, and of ideas, with which we are occupied every day. And without understanding them, how can the mind seek reality? It can invent 'reality', it can copy, it can imitate; because it has read so many books, it can repeat the experience of others. But surely that is not the real. To experience the real, the mind must cease to create, because whatever it creates is still within the bondage of time. The problem is not whether there is or is not God, but how man may discover God. If in his search he disentangles himself from everything, he will inevitably find that reality. But he must begin with the near and not with the far. Obviously, to go far one must begin near. But most of us want to speculate, which is a very convenient escape. That is why religions offer such a marvellous drug for most people.

So the task of disentangling the mind from all the values that it has created is an extremely arduous one, and because our minds are weary, or we are lazy, we prefer to read religious books and speculate about God; but that, surely, is not the discovery of reality. Realizing is experiencing, not imitating.

Q: Is the mind different from the thinker?

K: Now, is the thinker different from his thoughts? Does the thinker exist without thoughts? Is there a thinker apart from thought? Stop thinking, and where is the thinker? Is the thinker of one thought different from the thinker of another thought? Is the thinker separate from his thought, or does thought create the thinker, who then identifies himself with thought when he finds it convenient, and separates himself when it is not convenient? That is, what is the 'I', the thinker? Obviously, the thinker is composed of various thoughts that have become identified as the 'me'. So the thoughts produce the thinker, not the other way round. If I have no thoughts, then there is no thinker; not that the thinker is different each time, but if there are no thoughts there is no thinker. So thoughts produce the thinker, as actions produce the actor. The actor does not produce actions.

❖

Q: My experience is that without the co-operation of the 'I', there is no perception.

K: We cannot talk of pure perception. Perception is always mixed up with the perceiver—it is a joint phenomenon. If we talk of perception, the perceiver is immediately dragged in. It is beyond our experience to speak of perceiving; we never have such an experience as perceiving. You may fall into a deep sleep, when the perceiver does not perceive himself; but in deep sleep there is neither perception nor perceiver. If you know a state in which the perceiver is perceiving himself without bringing in other objects of perception, then only can you validly speak of the perceiver. As long as that state is unknown, we have no right to talk of the perceiver as apart from perception. So the perceiver and the perception are a joint phenomenon, they are the two sides of the same medal. They are not separate, and we have no right to separate two things that are not separate. We insist on separating the perceiver from the perception when there is no valid ground for it. We know no perceiver without perception, and we know no perception without a perceiver. Therefore, the only valid conclusion is that perception and perceiver, the 'I' and the will, are two sides of the same medal; they are two aspects of the same phenomenon, which is neither perception nor perceiver. But an accurate examination of it requires close attention.

Q: Where does that take us?

K: Sir, this question arose out of the inquiry about the search for God. Obviously, most of us want to know the experience of reality. Surely it can be known only when the experiencer stops experiencing, because the experiencer is creating the experience. If the experiencer is creating the experience, then he will create God; therefore it will not be God. Can the experiencer cease? That is the whole point in this question. Now if the experiencer and the experience are a joint phenomenon, which is so obvious, then the experiencer, the actor, the thinker, has to stop thinking. Is that not obvious? So can the thinker cease to think? Because when he thinks, he creates, and what he creates is not the real. Therefore to find out whether there is or there is not reality, God, or what you will, the thought process has to come to an end, which means that the thinker must cease—whether he is produced by thoughts is irrelevant for the moment. The whole thought process, which includes the thinker, has to come to an end. It is only then that we will find reality. Now, first of all, in bringing that process to an end, how is it to be done, and who is to do it? If the thinker does it, the thinker is still the product of thought. The thinker putting an end to thought is still the continuity of thought. So what is the thinker to do? Any exertion on his part is still the thinking process. I hope I am making myself clear.

❖

Q: Why do we insist on separating the perceiver from the perception, the rememberer from the memory? Is this not at the root of our trouble?

K: We separate it because the rememberer, the experiencer, the thinker, becomes permanent by separation. Memories are obviously fleeting; so the rememberer, the experiencer, the mind, separates itself because it wants permanency. The mind that is making an effort, that is striving, that is choosing, that is disciplined, obviously cannot find the real; because, as we said, through that very effort it projects itself and sustains the thinker. Now, how to free the thinker from his thoughts? This is what we are discussing. Because whatever he thinks must be the result of the past, and therefore he creates God, truth, out of memory, which is obviously not real. In other words, the mind is constantly moving from the known to the known. When memory functions, the mind can move only in the field of the known, and when it moves within the field of the known, it can never know the unknown. So our problem is how to free the mind from the known. To free ourselves from the known, any effort is detrimental because effort is still of the known. So all effort must cease. Have you ever tried to be without effort? If I understand that all effort is futile, that all effort is a further projection of the mind, of the 'I', of the thinker, if I realize the truth of that, what happens? If I see very clearly the label 'poison' on a bottle, I leave it alone. There is no effort not to be attracted to it. Similarly— and in this lies the greatest difficulty—if I realize that any effort on my part is detrimental, if I see the truth of that, then I am free of effort. Any effort on our part is detrimental, but we are not sure, because we want a result, we want an achievement—and that is our difficulty. Therefore, we go on striving, striving, striving. But God, truth, is not a result, a reward, an end. Surely it must come to us, we cannot go to it. If we make an effort to go to it, we are seeking a result, an achievement. But for truth to come, a man must be passively aware. Passive awareness is a state in which there is no effort; it is to be aware without judgment, without choice, not in some ultimate sense, but in every way; it is to be aware of your actions, of your thoughts, of your relative responses, without choice, without condemnation, without identifying or denying, so that the mind begins to understand every thought and every action without judgment. This evokes the question of whether there can be understanding without thought.

Q: Surely if you are indifferent to something . . .

K: Sir, indifference is a form of judgment. A dull mind, an indifferent mind, is not aware. To see without judgment, to know exactly what is happening, is awareness. So it is vain to seek God or truth without being aware now, in the immediate present. It is much easier to go to a temple, but that is an escape into the realm of speculation. To understand reality, we must know it directly, and reality is obviously not of time and space; it is in the present, and the present is our own thought and action.

Bombay, 8 February 1948

Questioner: Can one love truth without loving man? Can one love man without loving truth? Which comes first?

Krishnamurti: Surely, sir, love comes first. Because to love truth you must know truth, and to know truth is to deny it. What is known is not truth because what is known is already encased in time; therefore it ceases to be truth. Truth is in constant movement and therefore cannot *be* measured in time or in words; it cannot be held in your fist. So to love truth is to know truth—you cannot love something that you do not know. But truth is not to be found in books, in idolatry, in temples. It is to be found in action, in living, in thinking; and so love comes first—which is obvious, the very search for the unknown is love itself, and you cannot search for the unknown without being in relationship with others. You cannot seek out reality, God, or what you will, by withdrawing into isolation. You can find the unknown only in relationship, only when man is related to man. Therefore the love of man is the search for reality.

Without loving man, without loving humanity, there cannot be a search for the real; because when I know you—at least when I try to know you in relationship—in that relationship I am beginning to know myself. Relationship is a mirror in which I am discovering myself, not my 'higher' self, but the whole, total process of myself. The 'higher' self and the 'lower' self are still within the field of the mind; and without understanding the mind, the thinker, how can I go beyond thought, and discover? The very relationship is the search for the real because that is the only contact I have with myself; therefore the understanding of myself in relationship is the beginning of life, surely. If I do not know how to love you, you with whom I am in relationship, how can I search for the real, and therefore love the real? Without you, I am not, am I? I cannot exist apart from you, I cannot be in isolation. Therefore in our relationship, in the relationship between you and me, I am beginning to understand myself; and the understanding of myself is the beginning of wisdom, is it not? Therefore the search for the real is the beginning of love in relationship. To love something you must know it, you must understand it, mustn't you? To love you I must know you, I must inquire, I must find out, I must be receptive to all your moods, your changes, and not merely enclose myself in my ambitions, pursuits, and desires. And in knowing you I am beginning to discover myself. Without you, I cannot be; and if I do not understand that relationship between you and me, how can there be love? And surely without love there is no search, is there? You cannot say that one must love truth; because to love truth, you must know truth. Do you know truth? Do you know what reality is? The moment you know something, it is already over, is it not? It is already in the field of time, therefore it ceases to be truth.

Our problem is: How can a dry heart, an empty heart, know truth? It cannot. Truth is not something distant. It is very near, but we do not know how to look for it. To look for it, we must understand relationship, not only with man but with nature, with ideas. I must understand my relationship with the earth and my relationship with ideation, as well as my relationship with you; and in order to understand, surely there must be openness. If I want to understand you, I must be open to you, I must be receptive, I must not withhold anything, there cannot be an isolating process. In understanding there is truth, and to understand there must be love; for without love, there cannot be understanding. So it is not man or truth that comes first, but love; and love comes into being only in understanding relationship, which means that one is open to relationship, and therefore open to reality. Truth cannot be invited, it must come to you. To search for truth is to deny truth. Truth comes to you when you are open, when you are completely without a barrier, when the thinker is no longer thinking, producing, manufacturing, when the mind is very still—not forced, not drugged, not mesmerized by words, by repetition. Truth must come. When the thinker goes after truth, he is merely pursuing his own gain. Therefore truth eludes him. The thinker can be observed only in relationship; and to understand there must be love. Without love, there is no search.

❖

Q: You never mention God. Has he no place in your teachings?

K: You talk a great deal about God, don't you? Your books are full of it. You build churches, temples, you make sacrifices, you do rituals, perform ceremonies, and you are full of ideas about God, are you not? You repeat the word, but your acts are not godly, are they? Though you worship what you call God, your ways, your thoughts, your existence, are not godly, are they? Though you repeat the word *God*, you exploit others, do you not? You have your gods—Hindu, Moslem, Christian, and all the rest of it. You build temples, and the richer you get, the more temples you build. (Laughter.) Don't laugh, you would do the same yourself—only you are still trying to become rich that is all.

So you are very familiar with God, at least with the word; but the word is not God, the word is not the thing. Let us be very clear on that point: The word is not God. You may use the word *God* or some other word, but God is not the word that you use. Because you use it, it does not mean that you know God; you merely know the word. I don't use that word for the very simple reason that you know it. What you know is not the real. And besides, to find reality, all verbal mutterings of the mind must cease, must they not? You have images of God, but the image is not God, surely. How can you know God? Obviously not through an image, not through a temple. To receive God, the unknown, the mind must be the unknown. If you pursue God, then you already know God, you know the end. You know what you are pursuing, don't you? If you seek God, you must know what God is; otherwise, you wouldn't seek him, would you? You seek him either according to your books, or according to your feelings, and your feelings are merely the response of memory. Therefore that which you seek is already created, either through memory or through hearsay, and that which is created is not the eternal—it is the product of the mind. If there were no books, if there were no gurus, no formulas to be repeated, you would only know sorrow and happiness, wouldn't you?—constant sorrow and misery, and rare moments of happiness. And then you would want to know why you suffer. You couldn't escape to God—but you would probably escape in other ways, and soon invent gods as an escape. But if you really want to understand the whole process of suffering, as a new man, a fresh man, inquiring and not escaping, then you will free yourself from sorrow, then you will find out what reality is, what God is. But a man in sorrow cannot find God or reality; reality can be found only when sorrow ceases, when there is happiness, not as a contrast, not as an opposite, but that state of being in which there are no opposites.

So the unknown, that which is not created by the mind, cannot be formulated by the mind. That which is unknown cannot be thought about. The moment you think about the unknown, it is already the known. Surely you cannot think about the unknown, can you? You can think only about the known. Thought moves from the known to the known; and what is known is not reality, is it? So, when you think and meditate, when you sit down and think about God, you only think about what is known, and what is known is in time; it is caught in the net of time, and is therefore not the real. Reality can come into being only when the mind is free from the net of time. When the mind ceases to create, there is creation. That is, the mind must be absolutely still, but not with an induced, a hypnotized stillness, that is merely a result. Trying to become still in order to experience reality is another form of escape. There is silence only when all problems have ceased. As the pool is quiet when the breeze stops, so the mind is naturally quiet when the agitator, the thinker, ceases. To put an end to the thinker, all the thoughts that he manufactures must be thought out. It is no good erecting a barrier, a resistance against thought, because thoughts must be felt out.

When the mind is still, reality, the indescribable, comes into being. You cannot invite it. To invite it, you must know it, and what is known is not the real. So the mind must be simple, unburdened by belief, by ideation. And when there is stillness, when there is no desire, no longing, when the mind is absolutely quiet with a stillness that is not induced, then reality comes. And that truth, that reality, is the only transforming agent; it is the only factor that brings a fundamental, radical revolution in existence, in our daily life. And to find that reality is not to seek it, but to understand the factors that agitate the mind, that disturb the mind itself. Then the mind is simple, quiet, still. In that stillness the unknown, the unknowable, comes into being. And when that happens, there is a blessing.

Bombay, 27 February 1955

I THINK MOST of us must be greatly concerned with the problem of action. When we are confronted with so many issues—poverty, over-population, the extraordinary development of machinery, industrialization, the sense of deterioration inwardly and outwardly—what is one to do? What is the duty or the responsibility of an individual in his relation to society? This must be a problem to all thoughtful people. The more intelligent, the more active one is, the more one wants to throw oneself into social reform of some kind or other. So what is one's real responsibility? I think this question can be answered fully and with vital significance only if we understand the whole purpose of civilisation, of culture.

After all, we have built the present society; it is the outcome of our individual relationships. Does this society fundamentally help man to find reality, God, or what name you will? Or is it merely a pattern that determines our response to an issue, or what kind of action we should take in our relationship to society? If the present culture, civilisation, does not help man to find God, truth, it is a hindrance; and if it is a hindrance, then every reform, every activity for its amelioration is a further deterioration, a further hindrance to the discovery of reality, which alone can bring about true action.

I think it is very important to understand this, and not merely be concerned with what kind of social reform or activity one should identify oneself with. Surely that is not the problem. The problem is obviously much deeper. One may very easily get lost in some kind of activity or social reform, and then it is a means of escape, a means of forgetting or sacrificing oneself through action; but I do not think that will solve our many problems. Our problems are much more profound and we need a profound answer, which I think we shall find if we can go into this question as to whether the culture we have at present—culture implying religion, the whole social and moral framework—helps man to find reality. If it does not, then the mere reformation of such a culture or civilisation is a waste of time; but if it is helpful to man in the true sense, then all of us must give our hearts completely to its reformation. On that, I think, the issue depends.

By culture we mean the whole problem of thought, do we not? With most of us, thought is the outcome of various forms of conditioning, of education, of conformity, of the pressures and influences to which it is subjected within the framework of a particular civilisation. At present our thought is shaped by society, and unless there is a revolution in our thinking, the mere reformation of a superficial culture or society seems to me a distraction, a factor that will ultimately bring about greater misery.

After all, what we call civilisation is a process of educating thought in the Hindu mould, in the Christian or the Communist mould, and so on. Can thinking so educated ever create a fundamental revolution? Will any pressure, any shaping of thought, bring about the discovery or the understanding of what is truth? Surely thought must free itself from all pressure, which means really from society, from all forms of influence, and thereby find out what is truth; then that very truth has an action of its own that will bring about an altogether different culture.

That is, does society exist for the unfolding of reality, or must one be free of society to find reality? If society helps man to find reality, then every kind of reformation within society is essential; but if it is a hindrance to that discovery, should not the individual break away from society and seek what is truth? It is only such a person who is truly religious, not the man who performs various rituals, or who approaches life through theological patterns. When the individual frees himself from society and seeks reality, does he not bring about in his very search a different culture?

I think this is an important issue because most of us are merely concerned with reformation. We see poverty, overpopulation, every form of disintegration, division, and conflict; and seeing all that, what is one to do? Should one start by joining a particular group, or by working for some ideology? Is that the function of a religious man? The religious man, surely, is he who seeks reality, and not the man who reads and quotes the Gita, or who goes to the temple every day. That is obviously not religion; it is merely the compulsion, the conditioning of thought by society. So what is the earnest man to do, the man who sees the necessity for and desires to bring about an immediate revolution? Shall he work for reformation within the framework of society? Society is a prison, and shall he merely reform the prison, decorating its bars and getting things done more beautifully within its walls? Surely the man who is very much in earnest, who is really religious, is the only revolutionary; there is no other, and such a man is he who is seeking reality, who is trying to find out what is God or truth.

Now what is to be the action of such a man? What shall he do? Shall he work within the present society, or shall he break away from it and not be concerned with society at all? The breaking away does not mean becoming a sannyasi, a hermit, isolating himself with peculiar hypnotic suggestions. And yet he cannot be a reformer, because it is a waste of energy, of thought, of creativity, for the earnest man to indulge in mere reformations. Then what shall the earnest man do? If he does not want to decorate the prison walls, remove a few bars, introduce a little more light, if he is not concerned with all that, and if he also sees the importance of bringing about a fundamental revolution, a radical change in the relationship between man and man—the relationship that has created this appalling society in which there are immensely rich people and those who have absolutely nothing, both inwardly and outwardly—

then what is he to do? I think it is important to put this question to oneself.

After all, does culture come into being through the action of truth, or is culture man-made? If it is man-made, it will obviously not lead you to truth. And our culture is man-made, because it is based on various forms of acquisitiveness, not only in worldly things, but also in the so-called spiritual things; it is the outcome of the desire for position in every form, self-aggrandizement, and so on. Such a culture obviously cannot lead man to the realization of that which is the supreme; and if I see that, what shall I then do? What will you do if you actually realize that society is an impediment? Society is not merely one or two activities, it is the whole structure of human relationship in which all creativeness has ceased, in which there is constant imitation; it is a framework of fear where education is mere conformity and in which there is no love at all, but merely action according to a pattern described as love. In this society the principal factors are recognition and respectability; that is what we are all striving for—to be recognized. Our capacities, our knowledge must be recognized by society so that we shall be somebodies. When he realizes all this and sees the poverty, the starvation, the fragmentation of the mind into various forms of belief, what is the earnest man to do?

If we really listen to what is being said, listen in the sense of wanting to find out what is truth, so that there is not the conflict of your opinion against my opinion, or your temperament opposed to mine, if we can set all that aside and try to find out what is truth, which requires love, then I think in that very love, in that sense of goodness we shall find the truth that creates a new culture. Then one is free of society, one is not concerned with the reformation of society. But to find out what is truth requires love, and our hearts are empty, for they are filled with the things of society. Being filled, we try to reform, and our reformation is without the perfume of love.

So what is a man to do who is earnest? Shall he seek truth, God, or what name you will, or shall he give his heart and mind to the improvement of society, which is really the improvement of himself? Do you understand? Shall he inquire into what is truth, or shall he improve the conditions of society, which is his own improvement? Shall he improve himself in the name of society, or shall he seek truth, in which there is no improvement at all? Improvement implies time, time to become, whereas truth has nothing to do with time, it is to be perceived immediately.

So the problem is extraordinarily significant, is it not? We may talk about the reformation of society, but it is still the reformation of oneself. And for the man who is seeking what is real, what is truth, there is no reformation of the self; on the contrary, there is the total cessation of the self, which *is* society. Therefore he is not concerned with the reformation of society.

The whole structure of society is based on a process of recognition and respectability; and surely, sirs, an earnest man cannot seek the reformation of society, which is the improvement of himself. In reforming society, in identifying himself with something good, he may think he is sacrificing himself, but it is still self-improvement. Whereas, for the man who is seeking that which is the supreme, the highest, there is no self-improvement; in that direction there is no improvement of the 'me', there is no becoming, there is no practice, no thought of 'I shall be'. This means really the cessation of all pressure on thought, and when there is no pressure on thought, is there thinking? The very pressure on thought is the process of thinking, thinking in terms of a particular society, or in terms of a reaction to that society; and if there is no pressure, is there thinking? It is only the mind that has not this movement of thought— which is the pressure of society—it is only such a mind that can find reality; and in seeking that which is the supreme, such a mind creates the new culture. That is what is necessary: to bring about a totally different kind of culture, not to reform the present society. And such a culture cannot arise unless the earnest man pursues completely, with total energy, with love, that which is real. The real is not to be found in any book, through any leader; it comes into being when thought is still, and that stillness cannot be bought by any discipline. Stillness comes when there is love.

In considering some of these questions, I think it is important that we should directly experience what is being said, and you cannot do that if you are merely concerned with an answer to the question. If we are to go into the problem together, we cannot have opinions about it—my theory against your theory—because theories and speculations are a hindrance to the understanding of a problem. But if you and I can quietly, hesitantly penetrate deeply into the problem, then perhaps we shall be able to understand it. Actually there is no problem. It is the mind that creates the problem. In understanding the problem one is understanding oneself, the operations of one's own mind. After all, a problem exists only when any issue or disturbance has taken root in the soil of the mind. And is not the mind capable of looking at an issue, of being awake to any disturbance, without letting that disturbance take root in the mind? The mind is like a sensitive film; it perceives, it feels various forms of reaction. But is it not possible to perceive, to feel, to react with love, so that the mind itself does not become the soil in which the reaction takes root and becomes a problem?

Questioner: You have said that total attention is good; what then is evil?

Krishnamurti: I wonder if there is such a thing as evil? Please, give your attention, go with me, let us inquire together. We say there is good and evil. There is envy and love, and we say that envy is evil and love is good. Why do we divide life, calling this 'good' and that 'bad', thereby creating the conflict of the opposites? Not that there is not envy, hate, brutality in the human mind and heart, an absence of compassion, love; but why do we divide life into the thing called 'good' and the thing called 'evil'? Is there not actually only one thing, which is a mind that is inattentive? Surely when there is complete attention, that is, when the mind is totally aware, alert, watchful, there is no such thing as evil or good; there is only an awakened state. Goodness then is not a quality, not a virtue, it is a state of love. When there is love there is neither good nor bad, there is only love. When you really love somebody you are not thinking of good or bad, your whole being is filled with that love. It is only when there is the cessation of complete attention, of love, that there comes the conflict between what I am and what I should be. Then that which I am is 'evil', and that which I should be is the so-called 'good'.

Is it at all possible not to think in terms of fragmentation, not to break life up into the good and the evil, not to be caught in this conflict? The conflict of good and evil is the struggle to become something. The moment the mind desires to become something, there must be effort, the conflict between the opposites. This is not a theory. You watch your own mind and you will see that the moment the mind ceases to think in terms of becoming something, there is a cessation of action—which is not stagnation; it is a state of total attention that is goodness. But that total attention is not possible as long as the mind is caught in the effort to become something.

Please do listen, not only to what I am saying, but to the operations of your own mind, and that will reveal to you with what extraordinary persistence thought is striving to become something, everlastingly struggling to be other than it is, which we call discontent. It is this striving to become something that is 'evil', because it is partial attention, it is not total attention. When there is total attention, there is no thought of becoming, there is only a state of being. But the moment you ask, 'How am I to arrive at that state of being, how am I to be totally aware?' you have already entered the path of 'evil' because you want to achieve. Whereas, if one merely recognizes that as long as there is becoming, striving, making an effort to be something, one is on the path of 'evil', if one is able to perceive the truth of that, just see the fact as it is, then one will find that that is the state of total attention; and that state is goodness, there is no strife in it.

Q: Great cultures have always been based on a pattern, but you speak of a new culture that is free of pattern. Is a culture without pattern ever possible?

K: Must not the mind be free of all patterns to find reality? And being free to find that which is real, will it not create its own pattern, which the present society may not recognize? Can the mind that is caught in a pattern, that thinks in a pattern, that is conditioned by society, find the immeasurable that has no pattern? This language that is being spoken, English, is a pattern developed through centuries. If there is the creativity that is free of patterns, then that creativity, that freedom can employ the technique of language; but through the technique, the pattern of language, reality can never be found. Through practice, through a particular kind of meditation, through knowledge, through any form of experience, all of which are within a pattern, the mind can never understand what is truth. To understand what is truth, the mind must free itself from patterns. Such a mind is a still mind, and then that which is creative can create its own activity. But you see, most of us are never free from patterns. There is never a moment when the mind is totally free from fear, from conformity, from this habit of becoming something, either in this world or in the psychological, spiritual world. When the process of becoming in any direction completely ceases, then that which is God, truth, comes into being and creates a new pattern, a culture of its own.

Q: The problem of the mind and the social problem of poverty and inequality need to be tackled and understood simultaneously. Why do you emphasize only one?

K: Am I emphasizing only one? And is there such a thing as the social problem of poverty and inequality, of deterioration and misery, apart from the problem of the mind? Is there not only one problem, which is the mind? It is the mind that has created the social problem; and having created the problem, it tries to solve it without fundamentally altering itself. So our problem is the mind, the mind that wants to feel superior and thereby creates social inequality, that pursues acquisition in various forms because it feels secure in property, in relationship, or in ideas, which is knowledge. It is this incessant demand to be secure that creates inequality, that is a problem that can never be solved until we understand the mind that creates the difference, the mind that has no love. Legislation is not going to solve this problem, nor can it be solved by the Communists or the Socialists. The problem of inequality can be solved only when there is love, and love is not just a word to be thrown about. The man that loves is not concerned with who is superior and who is inferior; to him there is neither equality nor inequality; there is only a state of being which is love. But we do not know that state, we have never felt it. So how can the mind that is wholly concerned with its own activities and occupations, that has already created such misery in the world and is going right on creating further mischief, destruction—how can such a mind bring about within itself a total revolution? Surely that is the problem. And we cannot bring about this revolution through any social reform, but when the mind itself sees the necessity of this total redemption, then the revolution is there.

We are always talking of poverty, inequality, and reformation because our hearts are empty. When there is love we shall have no problems, but love cannot come into being through any practice. It can come into being only when you cease to be, that is, when you are no longer concerned about yourself, your position, your prestige, your ambitions and frustrations, when you stop thinking about yourself completely, not tomorrow but now. This occupation with oneself is the same, whether it be that of the man who is pursuing what he calls God, or that of the man who is working for a social revolution. And a mind so occupied can never know what love is.

Q: Tell us of God.

K: Instead of my telling you what God is, let us find out whether you can realize that extraordinary state, not tomorrow or in some distant future, but right now as we are quietly sitting here together. Surely that is much more important. But to find out what God is, all belief must go. The mind that would discover what is true cannot believe in truth, cannot have theories or hypotheses about God. Please listen. You have hypotheses, you have beliefs, you have dogmas, you are full of speculations. Having read this or that book about what truth or God is, your mind is astonishingly restless. A mind that is full of knowledge is restless; it is not quiet, it is only burdened, and mere heaviness does not indicate a still mind. When the mind is full of belief, either believing that there is God or that there is not God, it is burdened, and a burdened mind can never find out what is true. To find out what is true, the mind must be free, free of rituals, of beliefs, of dogmas, knowledge, and experience. It is only then that the mind can realize that which is truth. Because such a mind is quiet, it no longer has the movement of going out, or the movement of coming in that is the movement of desire. It has not suppressed desire, which is energy. On the contrary, for the mind to be still there must be an abundance of energy; but there cannot be ripeness or fullness of energy if there is any form of outward movement, and thereby a reaction inward. When all that has calmed down, the mind is still.

I am not mesmerizing you to be still. You yourself must see the importance of relinquishing, putting away without effort, without resistance, all the accumulations of centuries, the superstitions, knowledge, beliefs; you must see the truth that any form of burden makes the mind restless, dissipates energy. For the mind to be quiet there must be an abundance of energy, and that energy must be still. And if you have really come to that state in which there is no effort, then you will find that energy, being still, has its own movement that is not the outcome of society's compulsion or pressure. Because the mind has abundant energy that is still and silent, the mind itself becomes that which is sublime. There is no experiencer of the sublime; there is no entity who says, 'I have experienced reality.' As long as there is an experiencer, reality cannot be, because the experiencer is the movement to gather experience or to liquidate experience. So there must be a total cessation of the experiencer.

Just listen to this. Don't make an effort, just see that the experiencer, which is the outward and inward movement of the mind, must come to an end. There must be a total cessation of all such movement, and that requires astonishing energy, not the suppression of energy. When the mind is completely still, that is, when energy is neither dissipated nor distorted through discipline, then that energy is love; then that which is real is not separate from that energy itself.

Bombay, 24 December 1958

THE INDIVIDUAL IS of the highest importance, even though society, religion, governments do not recognize that fact. You are very important because you are the only means of bringing about the explosive creativity of reality. You yourself are the environment in which this reality can come into being. But you will have observed that all governments, all organized religions and societies, though they assert the importance of the individual, try to obliterate the individual core, the individual feeling, because they want collective feeling, they want a mass reaction. But the mind that is merely organized according to a certain pattern of belief, weighed down by custom, by tradition, by knowledge, is not an individual mind. An individual mind can only be when you deliberately, knowingly, with feeling, put all these influences aside because you have understood their significance, their superficial value. Then only is there an individual creative mind.

It is extraordinarily difficult to separate the individual from the mass, and yet without this separation reality is not possible. So the true individual is not the individual who merely has his own name, certain emotional responses, certain customary reactions, some property, and so on, but the true individual is he who is endeavouring to cut through this confusion of ideas, through this morass of tradition, who sets aside all these and tries to find the reason, the core, the centre of human misery. Such a one does not resort to books, to authority, to well-known custom, but casts all these away and begins to inquire—and he is the true individual. But most of us repeat, accept, comply, imitate, obey—do we not?—because for us obedience has become the rule—obedience in the home, obedience to the book, obedience to the guru, the teacher, and so on—and with obedience we feel there is security, safety. But actually life is not safe, life is never secure; on the contrary, it is the most uncertain thing. And because it is uncertain it is also profoundly rich, immeasurable. But the mind in its search seeks safety and security, and therefore it obeys, complies, and imitates; and such a mind is not an individual mind at all.

Most of us are not individuals though we each have a separate name, a separate form, because inwardly the state of mind is time-bound, weighed down by custom, tradition, and authority—the authority of the government, the authority of society, the authority in the home. Such a mind is not an individual mind; the individual mind is outside of all that; it is not within the pattern of society. The individual mind is in revolt and so is not seeking security. The revolutionary mind is not the mind that is in revolt. The revolutionary mind merely wants to alter things according to a certain pattern, and such a mind is not a mind in revolt, a mind that is in itself discontented.

I do not know if you have noticed what an extraordinary thing discontent is. You must know many young people who are discontented. They do not know what to do; they are miserable, unhappy, in revolt, seeking this, trying that, asking questions everlastingly. But as they grow older they find a job, marry, and that is the end of it. Their fundamental discontent is canalized, and then misery sets in. When they are young their parents, teachers, society, all tell them not to be discontented, to find out what they want to do and do it—but always within the pattern. Such a mind is not truly in revolt, and you need a mind in real revolt to find truth, not a conforming mind. Revolt means passion.

So it is very important to become an individual, and there is individuality only through self-knowledge—knowing yourself, knowing why you imitate, why you conform, why you obey. You obey through fear, do you not? Because of the desire to be secure you conform, in order to have more power, more money, or this or that. But to find what you call God, to find whether there is or is not that reality, there must be the individual who is dead to the past, who is dead to knowledge, dead to experience; there must be a mind that is wholly, totally new, fresh, innocent. Religion is the discovery of what is real, which means that you have to find, and not follow somebody who says he has found and wants to tell you about it. There must be a mind that receives that reality, not a mind that merely accepts reality verbally and conforms to that idea of reality in the hope of being secure.

So there is a difference between knowing and feeling, and I think it is very important to understand this. With us, explanations are sufficient, which is, 'to know'. We say: 'I know I am ambitious, I know I am greedy, I know I hate', but such knowing is not being free from the fact. You may know that you hate, but the actual feeling of hate and the freedom from it is an entirely different thing from the pursuit of the explanation of it and the cause of it, is it not? That is, to know that I am dull, stupid, and to be consciously aware of the feeling of my dullness and stupidity are two entirely different things. To feel implies a great deal of vitality, a great deal of strength, vigour, but merely to know is only a partial approach to life, it is not a total approach. You may know how a leaf is constructed, botanically, but to feel a leaf, smell it, really see it, requires a great deal of penetration—penetration into oneself. I do not know if you have ever taken a leaf in your hand and looked at it. You are all town-dwellers and you are all too occupied with yourselves, with your progress, with your success, ambitions, jealousies, your leaders, your ministers, and all the rest of the nonsense. It is tragic because if you knew how to feel deeply then you would have abundant sympathy, then you would do something, then you would act with your whole being; but if you merely know that there is poverty, merely work intellectually to remove poverty, as a government official or village reformer, without the feeling, then what you do is of very little importance.

You know, passion is necessary to understand truth—I am using the word *passion* in its full significance—because to feel strongly, to feel deeply, with all your being, is essential; otherwise that strange thing called reality will never come to you. But your religions, your saints say that you must not have desire, you must control, suppress, overcome, destroy, which means that you come to truth burnt out, worn out, empty, dead. You must have passion to meet this strange thing called life, and you cannot have passion, intense feeling, if you are mesmerized by society, by custom, if you are entangled in beliefs, dogmas, rituals. So to understand that light, that truth, that immeasurable reality, we must first understand what we call religion and be free of it—not verbally, not intellectually, not through explanations, but actually be free; because freedom—not your intellectual freedom but the actual state of freedom—gives vitality. When you have walked through all this rubbish, when you have put aside all these confusing, traditional, imitative things, then the mind is free, then the mind is alert, then the mind is passionate. And it is only such a mind that can proceed.

So let us, as individual human beings, because it is you and I who are concerned, not the mass—there is no such thing as the mass except as a political entity—let us find out what we mean by religion. What is it for most of us? Is it not a belief in something, in a superhuman divinity who controls us, shapes us, gives us hope and directs us? And we offer to that entity our prayers, our rituals; in its name we sacrifice, propitiate, pray, and beg, and we look to 'Him' as our 'Father' to help us in our difficulties. To us, religion is not only the graven image in the temple, the letters in the mosque, or the cross in the church, not only the graven image made by the hand, but also the graven image made by the mind, the idea. So to us, religion is obviously a means of escape from our daily sorrow, our daily confusion. We do not understand the inequalities, the injustices, death, the constant sorrows, struggles, hopelessness, and despair, so we turn to some god, to rituals, mass, prayers, and thereby hope to find some solace, some comfort. And in this process, the saints, the philosophers, the books weigh us down with their particular interpretation, with custom, with tradition. That is our way of

life, is it not? If you look into yourself wouldn't you agree that that
is a general outline of religion? It is a thing made by the mind for the
comfort of the mind, not something that gives richness, fullness of
life, or a passion for living. So we know that—but here again knowing and feeling are two different things. Knowing the falseness of organized religion is one thing, but to see it, to drop it, to put it all
away—that requires a great depth of real feeling. So the problem—
for which there is no easy answer—is how to drop a thing, how to die
to it, how to die to all these explanations, all these false gods; because all gods made by the mind and the hand are false. No explanation is going to make you die to it.

So what will make you die to it, what will make you say:
'Now, I drop it'? We generally give up something in order to get
something else we think is better, and we call it renunciation. But
surely that is not renunciation. To renounce means to give up not
knowing what the future is, not knowing what tomorrow will bring.
If you give up, knowing what tomorrow will bring, then it is merely
an exchange, a thing of the market; it has no value. When physical
death comes, you do not know what is going to happen next; it is a
finality. In the same way, to die, to give up, put aside totally, deeply,
all that we call religion, without knowing what will be—have you
ever tried this? I do not know if it is a problem to you, but it must
surely be a problem to anyone who is alert, who is at all aware, because there is such immense injustice in the world. Why does one
ride in a car while the other walks? Why is there hunger, poverty,
and also immense riches? Why is there the man in power, authority, position, wielding his power with cruelty? Why does a child die?
Why is there this intolerable misery everywhere? A man who asks all
these questions must be really burning with them, not finding some
stupid cause—an economic, social, or political cause. Obviously the
intelligent man must turn to something much more significant than
mere explanatory causes. And this is where our problem lies.

The first and most important thing is not to be satisfied by
explanations, not to be satisfied by the word *karma*, not to be satisfied with cunning philosophies, but to realize, to feel completely
that there is this immense problem that no mere explanation can

wipe away. If you can feel like that, then you will see that there is a revolution in the mind. Usually if one cannot find a solution to misery, one becomes bitter, cynical, or one invents a philosophical theory based on one's frustration. But if I am faced with the fact of suffering, that there is death, deterioration, and if the mind is stripped of all explanations, all solutions, all answers, then the mind is directly confronted with the thing itself; and curiously, our mind never allows that direct perception.

So there is a difference between seeing and knowing, feeling and loving. Feeling and loving does not mean devotion; you cannot get to reality through devotion. Giving yourself up emotionally to an idea is generally called devotion, but it excludes reality, because by giving yourself up to something you are merely identifying yourself with that thing. To love your gods, to put garlands around your guru, to repeat certain words, get entranced in his presence, and to shed tears—you can do all that for the next thousand years but you will never find reality. To perceive, to feel, to love a cloud, a tree, a human being, requires enormous attention, and how can you attend when your mind is distracted by knowledge? Knowledge is useful technologically, and that is all. If a doctor does not know how to operate, it is better to keep away from him. Knowledge is necessary at a certain level, in a certain direction, but knowledge is not the total answer to our misery. The total answer lies in this feeling, this passion that comes when there is the absence of yourself, when you are oblivious of all that you are. That quality of passion is necessary in order to feel, to understand, to love.

Reality is not intellectual; but from our childhood, through education, through every form of so-called learning we have brought about a mind that is sharp, that competes, that is burdened with information—which is the case with lawyers, politicians, technologists, and specialists. Our minds are sharpened, made bright, and that has become the most important thing to keep going; and so all our feeling has withered away. You do not feel for the poor man in his wretchedness; you never feel happy when you see a rich man driving in his beautiful car; you never feel delighted when you see a nice face; there is no throb when you see a rainbow or the splendour of the green grass. We are so occupied with our jobs, our own miseries, that we have never a moment of leisure in which to feel what it is to love, to be kind, to be generous. Yet without all this we want to know what God is! How incredibly stupid and infantile! So it becomes very important for the individual to come alive—not to revive; you cannot revive dead feelings, the glory that has gone. But can we not live intensely, fully, in abundance, even for a single day? For one such day covers a millennium. This is not a poetical fancy. You will know of it when you have lived one rich day in which there is no time, no future, no past; you will know then the fullness of that extraordinary state. Such living has nothing to do with knowledge.

Bombay, 8 March 1961

I CANNOT SEE anything, I cannot observe clearly, precisely, when I call myself a Hindu, a Christian, a Buddhist—which is the whole tradition, the weight of knowledge, the weight of conditioning. With that mind I can only look at life, at something as a Christian, as a Buddhist, as a Hindu, as a nationalist, as a Communist, as something or other; and that state prevents me from observing. That is simple.

When the mind watches itself as a conditioned entity, that is one state. But when the mind says, 'I am conditioned', that is another state. When the mind says, 'I am conditioned', in that state of the mind there is the 'I' as the observer watching the conditioned state. When I say, 'I see the flower', there is the observer and the observed; the observer is different from the thing observed; therefore there is distance, there is a time-lag, there is duality, there are the opposites; and then there is the overcoming of the opposites, the cementing of the dual. That is one state. Then there is the other state—when the mind observes itself as being conditioned—in which there is no observer and the thing observed. You see the difference?

❖

CAN YOUR MIND be aware that it is conditioned not as observer watching itself being conditioned—experiencing now, not tomorrow, not the next minute, the state in which there is no observer—the same as the state you experience when you are angry?

This demands tremendous attention. Not concentration; when you concentrate, there is duality. When you concentrate upon something, the mind is concentrated, watching the thing concentrated upon; therefore there is duality. In attention there is no duality because in that state there is only the state of experiencing.

When you say, 'I must be free from all conditioning, I must experience', there is still the 'I' who is the centre from which you are observing; therefore, in that there is no escape at all because there is always the centre, the conclusion, the memory, a thing that is watching, saying 'I must, I must not'. When you are looking, when you are experiencing, there is the state of the non-observer, a state in which there is no centre from which you look. At the moment of actual pain, there is no 'I'. At the moment of tremendous joy, there is no observer; the heavens are filled, you are part of it, the whole thing is bliss. This state of mind takes place when the mind sees the falseness of the state of mind that attempts to become, to achieve, and that talks about timelessness. There is a state of timelessness only when there is no observer.

Questioner: The mind that has observed its own conditions, can it transcend thought and duality?

Krishnamurti: You see how you refuse to observe something very simple? Sir, when you get angry, is there an idea in that state, is there a thought, is there an observer? When you are passionate, is there any other fact except that? When you are consumed with hatred, is there the observer, the idea, and all the rest of it? It comes later on, a split-second later, but in that state there is nothing of this.

Q: There is the object towards which love is directed. Is there duality in love?

K: Sir, love is not directed to something. The sunshine is not directed to you and me; it is there.

The observer and the observed, the idea and the action, the 'what is' and 'what should be'—in this, there is duality, the opposites of duality, the urge to correlate the two; the conflict of the two is in that field. That is the whole field of time. With that mind, you cannot approach or discover if there is time or if there is not. How is it possible to wipe that away? Not 'how', not a system, not a method, because the moment you apply a method you are again in the field of time. Then the problem is: Is it possible to jump away from that? You cannot do it by gradation, because that again involves time. Is it possible for the mind to wipe away the conditioning, not through time but by direct perception? This means the mind has to see the false and to see what is truth. When the mind says, 'I must find out what is timeless', such a question for a mind involved in time has no answer. But can the mind that is the product of time wipe itself away—not through effort, not through discipline? Can the mind wipe the thing away without any cause? If it has a cause then you are back again in time.

So you begin to inquire into what love is, negatively, as I explained before. Obviously love that has a motive is not love. When I give a garland to a big man because I want a job, because I want something from him, is that respect, or is it really disrespect? The man who has no disrespect is naturally respectful. It is a mind that is in a state of negation—which is not the opposite of the positive, but the negation of seeing what is false, and putting away the false as a false thing—that can inquire.

When the mind has completely seen the fact that through time, do what it will, it can never find the other, then there is the other. It is something much vaster, limitless, immeasurable; it is energy without a beginning and without an end. You cannot come to that, no mind can come to that, it has only 'to be'. We must only be concerned with the wiping away—if it is possible to wipe it clean—not gradually. That is innocency. It is only an innocent mind that can see this thing, this extraordinary thing that is like a river. You know what a river is? Have you watched up and down in a boat,

swum across a river? What a lovely thing it is! It may have a beginning and it may have an end. The beginning is not the river and
the end is not the river. The river is the thing in between; it passes
through villages; everything is drawn into it; it passes through towns,
all polluted with bad chemicals; filth and sewage is thrown into it;
and a few miles further, it has purified itself; it is the river in which
everything lives—the fish below and on top the man that drinks its
water. That is the river; but behind that, there is that tremendous
pressure of water, and it is this self-purificatory process that is the
river.

The innocent mind is like that energy. It has no beginning
and no end. It is God. Not the temple God. There is no beginning
and no end, therefore there is no time and timeless. And the mind
cannot come to it. The mind that measures in time must wipe itself away and enter into that without knowing that; because you cannot know it, you cannot taste it; it has no colour, no space, no shape.
That is for the speaker, not for you, because you have not left the
other. Don't say there is that state—it is a false state when that state-
ment is made by a person who is being influenced. All that you can
do is to jump out of it, and then you will know. Then you won't
even know: You are part of this extraordinary state.

London, 23 October 1949

EXPERIENCE IS NOT a measure, is not the way to reality because, after all, we experience according to our belief, according to our conditioning, and that belief is obviously an escape from ourselves. To know myself, I need not have any belief; I only have to watch myself clearly and choicelessly—watch myself in relationship, watch myself in escape, watch myself in attachment. One has to watch oneself without any prejudice, without any conclusion, without any determination. In that passive awareness, one discovers this extraordinary sense of aloneness. I am sure most of you have felt this—the sense of complete emptiness that nothing can fill. It is only in abiding in that state when all values have utterly ceased, only when we are capable of being alone and facing that aloneness without any sense of escape, only then that reality comes into being. Because values are merely the result of our conditioning; like experience, they are based on a belief, and are a hindrance to the understanding of reality.

But that is an arduous task that most of us are unwilling to go through. So we cling to experiences, mystical, superstitious, the experiences of relationship, of so-called love, and the experiences of possession. These become very significant, because it is of these that we are made. We are made of beliefs, of conditionings, of environmental influences. That is our background, and from that background, we judge, we value. And when one goes through, understands, the whole process of this background, then one comes to a point where one is utterly alone. One must be alone to find reality—which does not mean escape, withdrawal from life. On the contrary it is the complete intensification of life because then there is freedom from the background, from the memory of the experiences of escape. In that aloneness, in that loneliness, there is no choice, there is no fear of what is. Fear arises only when we are unwilling to acknowledge or see what is.

Therefore, it is essential, for reality to come into being, to set aside the innumerable escapes that one has established, in which one is caught up. If you observe, you will see how we use people—how we use our husbands and wives, or groups, or nationalities—to escape from ourselves. We seek comfort in relationship. Such a search for comfort in relationship brings certain experiences and to those experiences we cling. To escape from ourselves, knowledge also becomes extraordinarily important; but knowledge is obviously not the way to reality. Mind must be completely empty and still for reality to come into being. But a mind that is rattling around with knowledge, addicted to ideas and beliefs, ever chattering, is incapable of receiving that which is.

Similarly, if we seek comfort in relationship, then relationship is an avoidance of ourselves. In relationship we want comfort, we want something to lean on, we want support, we want to be loved, we want to be possessed—which all indicates the poverty of our own being. Similarly our desire for property, for name, for titles, for possessions, indicates that inward insufficiency.

When one realizes that this is not the way to reality, then one comes to that state when the mind is no longer seeking comfort, when the mind is completely content with what is—which does not mean stagnation. In the flight from what is there is death; in the recognition and awareness of what is there is life. So experience based on conditioning, the experience of a belief—which is the result of escape from ourselves—and the experience of relationship, these become a hindrance, a block; they cover up our insufficiencies. And it is only when we recognize that these things are an escape, and therefore see their true value, that there is a possibility of remaining quiet, still, in that emptiness, in that loneliness. And when the mind is very quiet, neither accepting nor rejecting, being passively aware of that which is, then there is a possibility for that immeasurable reality to be.

Questioner: Is there, or is there not, a divine plan? What is the sense of our striving if there is not one?

Krishnamurti: Why do we strive? And what are we striving after? What would happen if we did not strive? Would we stagnate and decay? What is this constant striving to be something? What does this strife, this effort, indicate? Does understanding come through effort, through striving? One is constantly striving to become better, to change oneself, to fit oneself to a certain pattern, to become something—from the clerk to the manager, from the manager to the divine. Does this striving bring understanding?

I think the question of effort should really be understood. What is it that is making the effort, and what do we mean by 'the will to be'? Don't we make an effort in order to achieve a result, in order to become better, in order to be more virtuous, or less of something else? There is this constant battle going on in us between positive and negative desires, one superseding the other, one desire controlling the other, only we call it the higher and the lower self. But obviously it is still desire. You can place it at any level, and give it a different name, it is still desire, a craving to be something. There is also the constant strife within oneself and with others, with society.

Now, does this conflict of desires bring understanding? Does the conflict of opposites, the want and the non-want, bring clarification? Is there understanding in the struggle to approximate ourselves to an idea? So the problem is not the strife, the struggle, or what would happen if we did not struggle, if we did not make an effort, if we did not strive to be something, psychologically as well as outwardly; the problem is: How does understanding come into being? Because when once there is understanding, there is no strife. What you understand, of that you are free.

How does understanding come into being? I do not know if you have ever noticed that the more you struggle to understand, the less you understand any problem. But the moment you cease to struggle and let the problem tell you the whole story, give all its significance, then there is understanding; which means, obviously, that to understand, the mind must be quiet. The mind must be choicelessly, passively, aware; and in that state, there is understanding of the many problems of our life.

The questioner wants to know if there is, or if there is not, a divine plan. I do not know what you mean by a 'divine plan', but we do know—do we not?—that we are in sorrow, that we are in confusion, that confusion and sorrow are ever on the increase, socially, psychologically, individually, and collectively. It is what we have made of this world. Whether there is a divine plan or not is not important at all. But what is important is to understand the confusion in which we live, outwardly as well as inwardly. To understand that confusion, we must begin, obviously, with ourselves, because we are confusion; it is we who have produced this outward confusion in the world. And to clear up that confusion we must begin with ourselves, because what we are the world is.

Now you will say, 'Well, it will take a very long time in this way to bring about order in the world.' I'm not at all sure that you are right; because, after all, it's one or two who are very clear, who understand, that bring about a revolution, a change. But we are lazy, you see, that is the difficulty. We want others to change, we want circumstances to change, we want the government to order our lives, or some miracle to take place that will transform us. And so we abide with confusion.

So what is really important is not to inquire if there is or if there is not a divine plan, because over that you will waste speculative hours, proving that there is or there is not. That becomes a game for the propagandists. What is important is really to free oneself from confusion, and that does not take a long period of time. What is essential is to see that one is confused, that all activity, all action that springs from confusion, must be confused also. It's like a confused person seeking a leader; his leader must also be confused. So what is essential is to see that one is confused, and not try to escape from it, not try to find explanations for it—to be passively, choicelessly, aware. Then you will see that quite a different action springs from that passive awareness. Because if you make an effort to clarify the state of confusion, what you create will still be confused. But if you are aware of yourself, choicelessly, passively aware, then that confusion unfolds and fades away.

You will see if you will experiment with this—and it will not take a long period of time, because time is not involved in it at all—that clarification comes into being. But you must give your whole attention, your whole interest, to it. I am not at all sure that most of us do not like to be confused because in the state of confusion you need not act. So we are satisfied with the confusion; because to understand confusion demands action that is not the pursuit of an ideal or an ideation.

So the question whether there is, or whether there is not, a divine plan is irrelevant. We have to understand ourselves and the world we have created: the misery, the confusion, the conflict, the wars, the divisions, the exploitations. All that is the result of ourselves in relationship with others. And if we can understand ourselves in relationship with others, if we can see how we use others, how we try to escape from ourselves through people, through property, through knowledge, and therefore give immense significance to relationship, to property, to knowledge—if we can see all that, be aware of it passively, then we shall be free from that background which we are. Then only is there a possibility of finding out what is. But to spend hours speculating whether there is a divine plan or not, striving to find out about it, lecturing about it, seems to me so infantile. For peace does not come into being through conformity to any plan, whether the plan is left, right, or divine. Conformity is mere suppression, and in suppression there is fear. Only in understanding can there be peace and tranquillity; and in that tranquillity, reality comes into being.

Q: Does understanding come to one suddenly, unrelated to past effort and experience?

K: What do we mean by past experience? How do you experience a challenge? After all, life is a process of challenge and response—is it not?—the challenge always being new, otherwise it is not a challenge. And our response is inevitably the outcome of the background, of our conditioning. So the response, if it is not adequate, full, complete, with regard to the challenge, must create friction, must create conflict. It is this conflict between the challenge and the response that we call experience. I do not know if you have ever noticed that if your response to the challenge is complete, there is only a state of experiencing, not the remembrance of an experience. But when the response is not adequate to the challenge, then we cling to the memory of the experience.

It is not so difficult, don't be so puzzled. Let us explore it a little more and you will see. As I said, life is a process of challenge and response—at all levels, not at one particular level—and as long as the response is not adequate to the challenge, there must be conflict. Surely that is obvious. And conflict invariably prevents understanding. Through conflict one cannot understand any problem, can one? If I am constantly quarrelling with my neighbour, with my wife, with my associates, it is not possible to understand that relationship. It is possible to understand only when there is no conflict.

Does understanding come suddenly? That is, can conflict cease suddenly? Or must one go through innumerable conflicts, understanding each conflict, and then be free of all conflict? That is, to put the problem differently, behind this question I'm sure there is another question: 'Since you have been through the various fogs, confusions, conflicts, belief in Masters, in reincarnation, the various societies, and so on, and so on, must I not also go through them? Since you have been through certain phases, must I not also go through those phases, in order to be free?' That is, must we not all experience confusion, in order to be free of confusion?

So isn't the question: 'Does understanding come through following or accepting certain patterns, and living through those patterns in order to be free?' Say, for example, at one time you believed in certain ideas, but now you have pushed them aside; you are free and have understanding. And I come along and see that you have lived through certain beliefs, and have pushed them aside and gained understanding. So I say to myself, 'I will also follow those beliefs, or accept those beliefs, and eventually I will come to understanding.' Surely that is a wrong process, is it not? What is important is to understand. Is understanding a matter of time? Surely not. If you are interested in something, there is no question of time. Your whole being is there, concentrated, completely absorbed in that thing. And it is only when you want to gain a result that the question of time comes in. So if you treat understanding as an end to be gained, then you require time, then you talk about 'immediate' or 'postponed'. But understanding, surely, is not an end-process. Understanding comes when you are quiet, when the mind is still. And if you see the necessity of the mind's being still, then immediately there is understanding.

Q: What, according to you, is true meditation?

K: Now what is the purpose of meditation? And what do we mean by meditation? I do not know if you have meditated, so let us experiment together to find out what is true meditation. Don't listen merely to my expression of it; together we will find out and experience what is true meditation. Because meditation is important, isn't it? If you do not know what is right meditation, there is no self-knowledge; and without knowing yourself, meditation has no meaning. To sit in a corner or walk about in the garden or in the street, and try to meditate, has no meaning. That only leads to a peculiar concentration that is exclusion. I'm sure some of you have tried all those methods. That is, you try to concentrate on a particular object, try to force the mind, when it is wandering all over the place, to be concentrated; and when that fails, you pray.

If one really wants to understand what right meditation is, one must find out what are the false things that we have called meditation. Obviously, concentration is not meditation because, if you observe, in the process of concentration there is exclusion, and therefore there is distraction. You are trying to concentrate on something, and your mind is wandering off towards something else; and there is a constant battle going on to be fixed on one point while the mind refuses and wanders off. So we spend years trying to concentrate, to learn concentration, which is mistakenly called meditation.

Then there is the question of prayer. Prayer obviously produces results, otherwise millions wouldn't pray. In praying, obviously, the mind is made quiet; by constant repetition of certain phrases the mind does become quiet. In that quietness there are certain intimations, certain perceptions, certain responses. But that is still a part of the trick of the mind; because, after all, through a form of mesmerism you can make the mind very quiet. And in that quietness there are certain hidden responses arising from the unconscious and from outside consciousness. But it is still a state in which there is no understanding.

And meditation is not devotion—devotion to an idea, to a picture, to a principle—because the things of the mind are still idolatrous. One may not worship a statue—considering that idolatrous, silly, superstitious—but one does worship, as most people do, the things of the mind. That is also idolatrous. To be devoted to a picture or an idea, to a Master, is not meditation. Obviously, it's a form of escape from oneself. It's a very comforting escape, but it's still an escape.

This constant striving to become virtuous, to acquire virtue through discipline, through careful examination of oneself, and so on, is obviously not meditation either. Most of us are caught in these processes, but since they do not give understanding of ourselves, they are not the way of right meditation. After all, without understanding yourself, what basis have you for right thinking? All that you will do without that understanding of yourself is to conform to the background, to the response of your conditioning. And such response to the conditioning is not meditation. But to be aware of those responses, that is, to be aware of the movements of thought and feeling without any sense of condemnation, so that the movements of the self, the ways of the self, are completely understood, that way is the way of right meditation.

Meditation is not a withdrawal from life. Meditation is a process of understanding oneself. And when one begins to understand oneself, not only the conscious but all the hidden parts of oneself as well, then there comes tranquillity. A mind that is made still, through meditation, through compulsion, through conformity, is not still. It is a stagnant mind. It is not a mind that is alert, passive, capable of creative receptivity. Meditation demands constant watchfulness, constant awareness of every word, every thought and feeling, which reveals the state of our own being, the hidden as well as the superficial; as that is arduous, we escape into every kind of comforting, deceptive thing, and call it meditation.

If one can see that self-knowledge is the beginning of meditation, then the problem becomes extraordinarily interesting and vital. Because if there is no self-knowledge, you may practise what you call meditation and still be attached to your principles, to your family, to your property; or, giving up your property, you may be attached to an idea, and be so concentrated on it that you create more and more of that idea. Surely that is not meditation. So self-knowledge is the beginning of meditation; without self-knowledge there is no meditation. And as one goes deeper into the question of self-knowledge not only does the upper mind become tranquil, quiet, but the different layers of the hidden are revealed. When the superficial mind is quiet, then the unconscious, the hidden layers of consciousness project themselves; they reveal their content, they give their intimations, so that the whole process of one's being is completely understood.

So the mind becomes extremely quiet—*is* quiet; it is not *made* quiet, it is not compelled to be quiet by a reward, by fear. Then there is a silence in which reality comes into being. But that silence is not Christian silence, or Hindu silence, or Buddhist silence. That silence is silence, not named. If you follow the path of Christian silence or Hindu or Buddhist, you will never be silent. A man who would find reality must abandon his conditioning completely— whether Christian, Hindu, Buddhist, or of any other group. Merely to strengthen the background through meditation, through conformity brings about stagnation of the mind, dullness of the mind; and I'm not at all sure that's not what most of us want, because it's so much easier to create a pattern and follow it. But to be free of the background demands constant watchfulness in relationship.

When once that silence is, then there is an extraordinary creative state—not that you must write poems, paint pictures; you may or you may not. But that silence is not to be pursued, copied, imitated—then it ceases to be silence. You cannot come to it through any path. It comes into being only when the ways of the self are understood, and the self with all its activities and mischief comes to an end. That is, when the mind ceases to create, then there is creation.

Therefore, the mind must become simple, must become quiet; it must *be* quiet—the 'must' is wrong; to say the mind *must* be quiet implies compulsion—and the mind is quiet only when the whole process of the self has come to an end. When all the ways of the self are understood, and therefore the activities of the self have come to an end, then only is there silence. That silence is true meditation. And in that silence the eternal comes into being.

Madras, 29 January 1964

I WOULD LIKE, if I may, to talk about meditation. I would like to talk about it because I feel it is the most important thing in life.

To understand meditation, to go into it very deeply, one must first of all understand the word and the fact; for most of us are slaves to words. The word *meditation* itself arouses in most people a certain state, a certain sensitivity, a certain quietness, a desire to achieve something or other. But the word is not the thing. The word, the symbol, the name—if it is not totally understood—is a terrible thing. It acts as a barrier, it makes the mind slavish. And the reaction to the word, to the symbol, makes most of us act, because we are unaware or unconscious of the fact itself. We come to the fact, to 'what is', with our opinions, judgments, evaluations, our memories. And we never see the fact, the 'what is'. I think that must be clearly understood.

To comprehend every experience, every state of mind, the 'what is', the actual fact, the actuality, one must not be a slave to words—and that is one of the most difficult things. The naming of it, the word, arouses various memories; and these memories impinge on the fact, control, shape, offer guidance to the fact, to the 'what is'. So, one must be extraordinarily aware of this confusion and not bring about a conflict between the word and the actuality, the 'what is'. And that is a very arduous task for a mind; that demands precision, clarity.

Without clarity, one cannot see things as they are. There is an extraordinary beauty in seeing things as they are—not from your opinions, your judgments, your memories. One has to see the tree as it is, without any confusion; similarly one has to see the sky on the water of an evening—just to see, without verbalization, without arousing symbols, ideas, and memories. In that there is extraordinary beauty. And beauty is essential. Beauty is the appreciation, the sensitivity to things about one—to nature, to people, to ideas. If there is no sensitivity, there will be no clarity; the two are together, synonymous. This clarity is essential if we would understand what meditation is.

A mind that is confused, a mind caught up in ideas, in experiences, in all the urges of desire, only breeds conflict. And a mind that would really be in a state of meditation has to be aware not only of the word, but also of the instinctive response of naming the experience or the state. And the very naming of that state or experience—whatever the experience be, however cruel, however real, however false—only strengthens memory with which we proceed to further experience.

Please, if I may point out, it is very important to understand what we are talking about, because if you do not understand this, you will not be able to take a journey with the speaker into this whole problem of meditation.

As we said, meditation is one of the most important things in life, or is, perhaps, the most important thing in life. If there is no meditation, there is no possibility of going beyond the limits of thought and mind and brain. And to go into this problem of meditation, from the very beginning one must lay the foundation of virtue. I do not mean the virtue imposed by society, a morality through fear, through greed, through envy, through certain punishment and reward. I am talking of virtue that comes about naturally, spontaneously, easily, without any conflict or resistance, when there is self-knowing. Without knowing yourself, do what you will, there cannot possibly be the state of meditation. I mean by 'self-knowing', knowing every thought, every mood, every word, every feeling, knowing the activity of your mind—not knowing 'the Supreme Self', 'the big Self'—there is no such thing, 'the Higher Self', 'the Atman', is still within the field of thought. Thought is the result of your conditioning, thought is the response of your memory—ancestral or immediate. And merely to try to meditate without first establishing deeply, irrevocably, that virtue that comes about through self-knowing, is utterly deceptive and absolutely useless.

Please, it is very important for those who are serious to understand this, because if you cannot do that, your meditation and actual living are divorced, are apart—so wide apart that though you may meditate, taking postures indefinitely, for the rest of your life, you will not see beyond your nose. Any posture you take, anything that you do, will have no meaning whatsoever.

So the mind that would inquire—I am using the word *inquire* purposely—into what meditation is, must lay this foundation that comes about naturally, spontaneously, with an ease of effortlessness, when there is self-knowing. And also it is important to understand what this self-knowing is, just to be aware, without any choice, of the 'me' that has its source in a bundle of memories—I will go presently into what we mean by awareness—just to be conscious of it without interpretation, merely to observe the movement of the mind. But that observation is prevented when you are merely accumulating through observation what to do, what not to do, what to achieve, what not to achieve. If you do that, you put an end to the living process of the movement of the mind as the self. That is, I have to observe and see the fact, the actual, the 'what is'. If I approach it with an idea, with an opinion—such as 'I must not' or 'I must', which are the responses of memory—then the movement of 'what is' is hindered, is blocked; and therefore there is no learning.

To observe the movement of the breeze in the tree you cannot do anything about it. It moves either with violence, or with grace, with beauty. You, the observer, cannot control it. You cannot shape it, you cannot say, 'I will keep it in my mind.' It is there. You may remember it. But if you remember it and recollect that breeze in the tree the next time you look at it, you are not looking at the natural movement of the breeze in the tree, but only remembering the movement of the past. Therefore you are not learning; you are merely adding to what you already know. So knowledge becomes, at a certain level, an impediment to a further level.

I hope this is very clear. Because what we are going into presently demands a mind that is completely clear, capable of looking, seeing, listening, without any movement of recognition.

So one must first be very clear, not confused. Clarity is essential. I mean by 'clarity', seeing things as they are, seeing the 'what is', without any opinion, seeing the movement of your mind, observing it very closely, minutely, diligently, without any purpose, without any directive. Just to observe demands astonishing clarity; otherwise, you cannot observe. If you observe an ant moving about, doing all the activities it does, by coming to it with various biological facts about the ant, that knowledge prevents you from looking. So you begin to see immediately where knowledge is necessary and where knowledge becomes an impediment. So there is no confusion.

When the mind is clear, precise, capable of deep, fundamental reasoning, it is in a state of negation. Most of us accept things so easily, we are so gullible because we want comfort, we want security, we want a sense of hope, we want somebody to save us— Masters, saviours, gurus, Rishis, you know the whole mess of it! We accept readily, easily; and equally easily we deny, according to the climate of our mind.

So 'clarity' is in the sense of seeing things as they are within oneself. Because oneself is a part of the world. Oneself is the movement of the world. Oneself is the outer expression of the movement that goes on inwardly—it is like the tide that goes out and comes in. Merely to concentrate on, or observe yourself, apart from the world, leads you to isolation and to all forms of idiosyncrasy, neurosis, isolating fears, and so on. But if you observe the world and follow the movement of the world, and ride that movement as it comes within, then there is no division between you and the world; then you are not an individual opposed to the collective.

And there must be this sense of observation that is both explorative and observing, listening and being aware. I am using the word *observing* in that sense. The very act of observation is the act of exploration. You cannot explore if you are not free. Therefore to explore, to observe, there must be clarity. To explore within yourself deeply, you must come to it each time afresh. That is, in that exploration you have never achieved a result, you have never climbed a ladder, and you never say, 'Now I know.' There is no ladder. If you do climb, you must come down immediately, so that your mind is tremendously sensitive to observe, to watch, to listen.

And out of this observing, listening, seeing, watching, comes that extraordinary beauty of virtue. There is no other virtue except that which comes from self-knowing. Then that virtue is vital, vigorous, active—not a dead thing that you cultivate. And that must be the foundation. The foundation for meditation is observation, clarity, and virtue, in the sense we mean—not in the sense of making virtue a thing to be cultivated day after day, which is mere resistance.

Then we can see from there the implications of the so-called prayers, the so-called repetition of words, mantras, sitting in a corner, and trying to fix your mind on a particular object, or a word, or a symbol—which is to meditate deliberately. Please listen carefully. Taking a deliberate posture or doing certain things to meditate, deliberately, consciously, only implies that you are playing in the field of your own desires and your own conditioning; therefore it is not meditation. One can see very well, if one observes, that those people who meditate have all kinds of images; they see Krishna, Christ, Buddha, and they think they have got something. Like a Christian seeing the Christ; that phenomenon is very simple, very clear; it is a projection of his own conditioning, his own fears, his own hopes, his desire for security. The Christian sees the Christ as you would see Rama or whatever your particular pet god is.

There is nothing remarkable about these visions. They are the product of your unconscious that has been so conditioned, so trained in fear. When you become slightly quiet, up it pops with its images, symbols, ideas. So visions, trances, pictures, and ideas have no value whatsoever. It is like a man repeating some mantra or some phrase or a name over and over and over again. When you repeat a name over and over and over again, obviously what happens is that you make the mind dull, stupid; and in that stupidity it becomes quiet. You can just as well take a drug to make the mind quiet— and there are such drugs—and in that state of quietness, in that drugged state, you have visions. Those are obviously the product of your own society, of your own culture, of your own hopes and fears; they have nothing whatsoever to do with reality.

Prayers are equally so. The man who prays is like a man who has his hand in another man's pocket. The businessman, the politician, and the whole competitive society are praying for peace; but they are doing everything to bring about war, hatred, and antagonism. It has no meaning, it has no rationality. Your prayer is a supplication, asking for something for which you have no right to ask—because you are not living, you are not virtuous. You want something peaceful, great, to enrich your lives, but you are doing everything opposite to destroy, becoming mean, petty, stupid.

Prayers, visions, sitting in a corner upright, breathing rightly, doing things with your mind, are so immature, juvenile; they have no meaning for a man who really wants to understand the full significance of what meditation is. So a man who would understand what meditation is puts all this aside completely, even though he may lose his job. He does not immediately turn to a petty god in order to get a new job—that is the game you all play. When there is some kind of sorrow, disturbance, you turn to a temple, and you call yourself religious! All these must be completely, totally set aside, so that they do not touch you. If you have done this, then we can proceed into this whole question of what is meditation.

You must have observation, clarity, self-knowing and, because of that, virtue. Virtue is a thing that is flowering in goodness all the time; you might make a mistake, do ugly things, but they are finished; you are moving, are flowering in goodness, because you are knowing yourself. Having laid that foundation, then you can put aside the prayers, the muttering of words and taking postures. Then you can begin to inquire into what experience is.

It is very important to understand what experience is, because we all want experience. We have everyday experiences—going to the office, quarrelling, being jealous, envious, brutal, competitive, sexual. In life, we go through every kind of experience, day after day, consciously or unconsciously. We are living on the surface of our life, without beauty, without any depth, with nothing of our own that is original, pristine, clear. We are all second-hand human beings, quoting others, following others, empty as a shell. And naturally we want more experience other than everyday experience. So we search for this experience either through meditation, or through taking some of the latest drugs. LSD25 is one of these latest drugs; the moment you have taken it, you feel you have 'instant mysticism'—not that I have taken it. (Laughter.)

We are talking seriously. You merely laugh at the least provocation; therefore you are not serious; you are not going step by step into it, watching yourself; you are just listening to words, going along riding on words—which I warned you against at the beginning of this.

There are these drugs that give you an expansion of consciousness, make you highly sensitive for the time being. And in that state of heightened sensitivity you see things: The tree becomes most astonishingly alive, bright and clear, and with an immensity. Or, if you are religiously minded, in that heightened state of sensitivity you have an extraordinary sense of peace and light; there is no difference between you and the thing observed—you are it, and the whole universe is part of you. And you crave for these drugs because you want more experience, a wider and deeper experience, hoping that experience will give significance to your life; so you begin to depend. Yet, when you have these experiences, you are still within the field of thought, within the field of the known.

So you have to understand experience—that is, the response to a challenge, which becomes a reaction; and that reaction shapes your thought, your feeling, your being. And you add more and more experiences; you think of having more and more experiences. The more clear the memories of those experiences are, the more you think you know. But if you observe, you will find that the more you know, the more shallow you become, the more empty. Becoming more empty, you want more and wider experience. So you have to understand not only all that I have said previously, but also this extraordinary demand for experience. Now we can proceed.

A mind that is seeking experience of any kind is still within the field of time, within the field of the known, within the field of self-projected desires. As I said at the beginning of this, deliberate meditation only leads to illusion. Yet there must be meditation. To meditate deliberately only leads you to various forms of self-hypnosis, to various forms of experience projected by your own desires, by your own conditioning; and those conditionings, those desires shape your mind, control your thought. So a man who would really understand the deep significance of meditation must understand the significance of experience; and also his mind must be free from seeking. That is very difficult. I am going to go into that presently.

Having laid all this as a basic thing, naturally, spontaneously, easily, then we must find out what it means to control thought. Because that is what you are after; the more you can control thought, the more you think you have advanced in meditation. For me, every form of control—physical, psychological, intellectual, emotional—is detrimental. Please listen carefully. Do not say, 'Then I will do what I like.' I am not saying that. Control implies subjugation, suppression, adaptation, shaping the thought to a particular pattern—which implies that the pattern is more important than the discovery of what is true. So control in any form—resistance, suppression, or sublimation—shapes the mind more and more according to the past, according to the conditioning in which you have been brought up, according to the conditioning of a particular community, and so on and on.

It is necessary to understand what meditation is. Now please listen carefully. I do not know if you have ever done this kind of meditation. Probably you have not, but you are going to do it now with me. We are going to take the journey together, not verbally, but actually go through it right up to the end of where verbal communication exists. It is like going together up to the door; then either you go through the door, or you stop on this side of the door. You will stop on this side of the door if you have not actually, factually, done everything that is being pointed out—not because the speaker says so, but because that is sane, healthy, reasonable, and it will stand every test, every examination.

So now, together, we are going to meditate—not deliberately meditate, because that does not exist. It is like leaving the window open and the air comes when it will—whatever the air brings, whatever the breeze is. But if you expect, wait for the breezes to come because you have opened the window, they will never come. So it must be opened out of love, out of affection, out of freedom— not because you want something. And that is the state of beauty, that is the state of mind that sees and does not demand.

To be aware is an extraordinary state of mind—to be aware of your surroundings, of the trees, the bird that is singing, the sunset behind you; to be aware of the faces, of the smiles; to be aware of the dirt on the road; to be aware of the beauty of the land, of a palm tree against the red sunset, the ripple of the water—just to be aware, choicelessly. Please do this as you are going along. Listen to these birds; do not name them, do not recognize the species, but just listen to the sound. Listen to the movement of your own thoughts; do not control them, do not shape them, do not say, 'This is right, that is wrong.' Just move with them. That is awareness in which there is no choice, no condemnation, no judgment, no comparison or interpretation, only mere observation. That makes your mind highly sensitive. The moment you name, you have gone back, your mind becomes dull, because that is what you are used to.

In that state of awareness there is attention—not control, not concentration. There is attention. That is, you are listening to the birds, you are seeing the sunset, you are seeing the stillness of the trees, you are hearing the cars go by, you are hearing the speaker;

and you are attentive to the meaning of the words, you are attentive to your own thoughts and feelings, and to the movement in that attention. You are attentive comprehensively, without a border, not only consciously, but also unconsciously. The unconscious is more important; therefore, you have to inquire into the unconscious.

I am not using the word *unconscious* as a technical term or a technique. I am not using it in the sense in which the psychologists use it but as that of which you are not conscious. Because most of us are living on the surface of the mind: going to the office, acquiring knowledge or a technique, quarrelling, and so on. We never pay attention to the depth of our being, which is the result of our community, of the racial residue, of all the past—not only of you as a human being, but also of man, the anxieties of man. When you sleep, all these project themselves as dreams, and then there is the interpretation of those dreams. Dreams become totally unnecessary for a man who is awake, alert, watching, listening, aware, attentive.

Now, this attention demands tremendous energy; not the energy that you have gathered through practice, being celibate and all the rest of that stuff—that is all the energy of greed. I am talking of the energy of self-knowing. Because you have laid the right foundation, out of that comes the energy to be attentive, in which there is no sense of concentration.

Concentration is exclusion—you want to listen to that music [from a nearby street], and you want also to hear what the speaker is saying, so you resist that music and try to listen to the speaker; so you are really not paying complete attention. A part of your energy has gone to resist that music and a part of it is trying to listen; therefore you are not listening totally; therefore you are not being attentive. So if you concentrate, you merely resist, exclude. But a mind that is attentive can concentrate and not be exclusive.

So out of this attention comes a brain that is quiet. The brain cells themselves are quiet—not made quiet, not disciplined, not enforced, not brutally conditioned. But because this whole attention has come into being naturally, spontaneously, without effort, easily, the brain cells are not perverted, not hardened, not coarsened, not brutalized. I hope you are following all this. Unless the brain cells themselves are astonishingly sensitive, alert, vital, not hardened, not beaten, not overworked, not specialized in a particular department of knowledge, unless they are extraordinarily sensitive, they cannot be quiet. So the brain must be quiet, but yet be sensitive to every reaction, be aware of all the music, the noises, the birds, hearing these words, watching the sunset—without any pressure, without any strain, without any influence. The brain must be very quiet, because without quietness—uninduced, not brought about artificially—there can be no clarity.

And clarity can only come when there is space. You have space the moment the brain is absolutely quiet but yet highly sensitive, not deadened. And that is why what you do all day is very important. The brain is brutalized by circumstances, by society, by your jobs and by specialization, by your thirty or forty years in an office, grinding away brutally—all that destroys the extraordinary sensitivity of the brain. And the brain must be quiet. From there, the whole mind, in which is included the brain, is capable of being completely still. That still mind is no longer seeking, it is not waiting for experience; it is not experiencing anything at all.

I hope you are understanding all this. Perhaps you aren't. It doesn't matter, just listen. Do not be mesmerized by me, but listen to the truth of this. And perhaps then, when you are walking in the street, sitting in a bus, watching a stream or a rice field, rich and green, this will come unknowingly, like a breath from a distant land.

So the mind then becomes completely still, without any form of pressure, compulsion. This stillness is not a thing produced by thought, because thought has ended, the whole machinery of thought has come to an end. Thought must end; otherwise, thought will produce more images, more ideas, more illusions—more and more and more. Therefore you have to understand this whole machinery of thought—not how to stop thinking. If you understand the whole machinery of thought, which is the response of memory, association and recognition, naming, comparing, judging—if you understand it, naturally it comes to an end. When the mind is completely still, then out of that stillness, in that stillness, there is quite a different movement.

That movement is not a movement created by thought, by society, by what you have read or not read. That movement is not of time, of experience because that movement has no experience. To a still mind there is no experience. A light that is burning brightly, that is strong, does not demand anything more, it is a light to itself. That movement is not a movement in any direction, because direction implies time. That movement has no cause, because anything that has a cause produces an effect and that effect becomes the cause and so on—an endless chain of causation and effect. So there is no effect, no cause, no motive, no sense of experiencing at all. Because the mind is completely still, naturally still, because you have laid the foundation, it is directly related to life, it is not divorced from everyday living.

If the mind has gone that far, that movement is creation. Then there is no anxiety to express, because a mind that is in a state of creation may express or may not express. That state of mind that is in that complete silence—it will move, it has its own movement into the unknown, into that which is unnameable.

So the meditation that you do is not the meditation of which we are talking. This meditation is from the everlasting to the everlasting, because you have laid the foundation not on time but on reality.

Madras, 15 December 1974

THE THINGS THAT thought has put together as sacred are not sacred. They are just words to give a significance to life, because life as you live is not sacred, is not holy. The word *holy* comes from being whole, which means healthy, sane—all that is implied in that word. So a mind that is functioning through thought, however desirous it be to find that which is sacred, is still acting within the field of time, within the field of fragmentation. Can that mind be whole, not fragmented? This is all part of the understanding of what meditation is. Can the mind that is the product of evolution, product of time, product of so much influence, so many hurts, so many travails, such great sorrow, great anxiety—caught in all that, all that is the result of thought, thought that is fragmentary by its very nature—can the mind that is the result of thought, as it is now, be free of the movement of thought? Can the mind be completely non-fragmented? Can you look at life as a whole? Can the mind be whole, which means without a single fragment? Therefore diligence comes into this. A mind is whole when it is diligent, which means having care, having great affection, great love—which is totally different from the love of a man and a woman.

So the mind that is whole is attentive, and therefore cares, and has this quality of a deep abiding sense of love. Such a mind is the whole that you come upon when you begin to inquire into what meditation is. Then we can proceed to find out what is sacred.

Please listen. It is your life. Give your heart and mind to find out a way of living differently, which means when the mind has abandoned all control. That does not mean to lead a life of doing what you like, yielding to every desire, to every lustful glance or re-action, to every pleasure, to every demand of the pursuit of pleasure, but to find out, to find out whether you can live a daily life without a single control. That is part of meditation. That means one has to have this quality of attention. That attention has brought about in-sight into the right place of thought and seen that thought is frag-mentary, and that where there is control, there is the controller and the controlled, which is fragmentary. So to find out a way of living without a single control, requires tremendous attention, great disci-pline. We are not talking of the discipline that you are accustomed to, which is merely suppression, control, conformity, but of a disci-pline that means to learn. The word *discipline* comes from the word *disciple*. The disciple is there to learn. Now here there is no teacher, no disciple; you are the teacher and you are the disciple if you are learning. That very act of learning brings about its own order.

Now thought has found its own place, its right place. So the mind is no longer burdened with the movement of thought as a ma-terial process, which means the mind is absolutely quiet. It is natu-rally quiet, not made quiet. That which is made quiet is sterile. In that which happens to be quiet, in that quietness, in that empti-ness, a new thing can take place.

Can the mind, your mind, be absolutely quiet, without con-trol, without the movement of thought? It will be quiet naturally if you really have the insight that brings about the right place for thought—thought has its right place, therefore the mind is quiet. You understand what the words *silence* and *quiet* mean? (You know you can make the mind quiet by taking a drug, by repeating a mantra or a word. By constantly repeating, repeating, repeating, naturally your mind will become quiet, but such a mind is a dull, stupid mind.) There is a silence between two noises. There is si-lence between two notes. There is silence between two movements of thought. There is silence of an evening when the birds have made their noise, chattering, and have gone to bed. When there isn't a flutter among the leaves, there is no breeze, there is absolute quietness. Not in a city, but when you are out with nature, when you are with the trees or sitting on the banks of the river, there silence descends on the earth and you are part of that silence. So there are different kinds of silence. But the silence we are talking about, the quietness of a mind, that silence is not to be bought, is not to be practised, is not something you gain as a reward, a compensation to an ugly life. It is only when the ugly life has been transformed into the good life—by good I mean not having plenty, but the life of goodness—in the flowering of that goodness, that beauty, then the silence comes.

You also have to inquire into what beauty is. What is beauty? Have you ever gone into this question? Will you find it in a book and tell me, or tell each other that book says what beauty is? What is beauty? Did you look at the sunset this evening as you are sitting there? The sunset was behind the speaker—did you look at it? Did you feel the light and the glory of that light on a leaf? Or do you think beauty is sensuous, and that a mind that is seeking sacred things cannot be attracted to beauty, cannot have anything to do with beauty, and therefore only concentrate on your little image that you have projected from your own thought as the good. If you want to find out what meditation is, you have to find out what beauty is, beauty in the face, beauty in character—not character, character is a cheap thing that depends on reaction to environment; the cultivation of that reaction is called character—the beauty of action, the beauty of behaviour, conduct, the inward beauty, the beauty of the way you walk, the way you talk, the way you gesture. All that is beauty and, without having that, meditation becomes merely an escape, a compensation, a meaningless action. There is beauty in frugality; there is beauty in great austerity—not the austerity of the sannyasi, the austerity of a mind that has order. Order comes when you understand the whole disorder in which you live, and out of that disorder comes naturally order that is virtue. Therefore virtue, order, is supreme austerity, not the denial of three meals a day or fasting, or shaving your head, and all the rest of that business.

So there is order, which is beauty. There is beauty of love, beauty of compassion. And also there is the beauty of a clean street, of good architectural form of a building; there is beauty of a tree, a lovely leaf, the great big branches. To see all that is beauty; not merely to go to museums and talk everlastingly about beauty. The silence of a quiet mind is the essence of that beauty. Because it is silent and because it is not the plaything of thought, then in that silence there comes that which is indestructible, which is sacred. In the coming of that which is sacred then life becomes sacred, your life becomes sacred, our relationship becomes sacred, everything becomes sacred because you have touched that thing that is sacred.

We have also to find out in meditation if there is something, or if there is nothing, that is eternal, timeless. Which means, can the mind that has been cultivated in the area of time, can that mind find out, come upon, or see that thing that is from everlasting to everlasting? It means, can the mind be without time? Though time is necessary to go from here to there and all the rest of it, can that mind, that very same mind that operates in time, going from here to there, not psychologically but physically, can that mind be without time? Which means can that mind be without the past, without the present, without the future? Can that mind be in absolute nothingness? Don't be frightened of that word. Because it is empty it has got vast space. Have you ever observed in your own mind if you have any space at all there? Just space, you know, a little space? Or is everything crowded? Crowded by your worries, by your sex, or no sex, by your achievements, by your knowledge, by your ambitions, fears, by your anxieties, your pettiness—crowded. How can such a mind understand, or be in that state of being or have that enormous space?

Space is always enormous. A mind that has no space in daily life cannot possibly come upon that which is eternal, that is timeless. That is why meditation becomes extraordinarily important. Not the meditation that you all practise, that is not meditation at all. The meditation of which we are talking transforms the mind. It is only such a mind that is the religious mind, and it is only such a religious mind that can bring about a different culture, a different way of life, different relationship, a sense of sacredness and therefore great beauty and honesty. All this comes naturally, without effort, without battle.

From Krishnamurti's Notebook

20 July 1961

THE ROOM BECAME full with that benediction. Now what followed
is almost impossible to put down in words; words are such dead
things, with definite set meaning, and what took place was beyond
all words and description. It was the centre of all creation; it was a
purifying seriousness that cleansed the brain of every thought and
feeling; its seriousness was as lightning that destroys and burns up;
the profundity of it was not measurable, it was there immovable, impenetrable, a solidity that was as light as the heavens. It was in the
eyes, in the breath. It was in the eyes and the eyes could see. The
eyes that saw, that looked were wholly different from the eyes of the
organ and yet they were the same eyes. There was only seeing, the
eyes that saw beyond time-space. There was impenetrable dignity
and a peace that was the essence of all movement, action. No virtue
touched it for it was beyond all virtue and sanctions of man. There
was love that was utterly perishable and so it had the delicacy of all
new things, vulnerable, destructible and yet it was beyond all this. It
was there imperishable, unnameable, the unknowing. No thought
could ever penetrate it; no action could ever touch it. It was 'pure',
untouched, and so ever dyingly beautiful.

All this seemed to affect the brain; it was not as it was before. (Thought is such a trivial thing, necessary but trivial.) Because

of it, relationship seems to have changed. As a terrific storm, a destructive earthquake gives a new course to the rivers, changes the landscape, digs deep into the earth, so it has levelled the contours of thought, changed the shape of the heart.

30 July 1961

It was a cloudy day, heavy with dark clouds; it had rained in the morning and it had turned cold. After a walk we were talking but more looking at the beauty of the earth, the houses, and the dark trees.

Unexpectedly, there was a flash of that unapproachable power and strength that was physically shattering. The body became frozen into immobility and one had to shut one's eyes not to go off into a faint. It was completely shattering and everything that was didn't seem to exist. And the immobility of that strength and the destructive energy that came with it, burned out the limitations of sight and sound. It was something indescribably great whose height and depth are unknowable.

Early this morning, just as dawn was breaking, with not a cloud in the sky and the snowcovered mountains just visible, woke up with that feeling of impenetrable strength in one's eyes and throat; it seemed to be a palpable state, something that could never not be there. For nearly an hour it was there and the brain remained empty. It was not a thing to be caught by thought and stored up in memory to be recalled. It was there and all thought was dead. Thought is functional, is only useful in that realm; thought could not think about it for thought is time and it was beyond all time and measure. Thought, desire could not seek for its continuation or for its repetition, for thought, desire, was totally absent. Then what is it that remembers to write this down? Merely a mechanical record but the record, the word is not the thing.

18 August 1961

It had been raining most of the night and it had turned quite cold; there was quite a lot of fresh snow on the higher hills and mountains. And there was a sharp wind too. The green meadows were extraordinarily bright and the green was startling. And it had been raining most of the day too and only towards the late afternoon it began to clear up and sun was amongst the mountains. We were walking along a path that went from one village to another, a path that wound around farmhouses, among rich green meadows. The pylons that carried heavy electric cables, stood startlingly against the evening skies; looking up at these towering steel structures against scudding clouds, there was beauty and power. Crossing over a wooden bridge, the stream was full, swollen by all this rain; it was running fast, with an energy and force that only mountain streams have. Looking up and down the stream, held in by tightly packed banks of rocks and trees, one was aware of the movement of time, the past, the present and future; the bridge was the present and all life moved and lived through the present.

But beyond all this, there was along that rain-washed and slushy lane, an otherness, a world that could never be touched by human thought, its activities and its unending sorrows. This world was not the product of hope nor of belief. One was not fully aware of it at that moment, there were too many things to observe, feel, and smell; the clouds, the pale blue sky beyond the mountains and the sun among them and the evening light on the sparkling meadows; the smell of cowsheds and red flowers around the farmhouses. This otherness was there covering all this, never a little thing being missed, and as one lay awake in bed, it came pouring in, filling the mind and the heart. Then one was aware of its subtle beauty, its passion and love. It's not the love that is enshrined in images, evoked by symbols, pictures, and words, nor that which is cloaked in envy and jealousy, but that which is there freed from thought and feeling, a curving movement, everlasting. Its beauty is there with the self-abandonment of passion. There's no passion of that beauty if there is no austerity. Austerity is not a thing of the mind, carefully gathered through sacrifice, suppression, and discipline. All these must cease, naturally, for they have no meaning for that otherness. It came pouring in with its measureless abundance. This love had no centre nor periphery and it was so complete, so invulnerable that there was no shadow in it and so ever destructible.

We always look from outside within; from knowledge we proceed to further knowledge, always adding and the very taking away is another addition. And our consciousness is made up of a thousand remembrances and recognitions, conscious of the trembling leaf, of the flower, of that man passing by, that child running across the field; conscious of the rock, the stream, the bright red flower, and the bad smell of a pigsty. From this remembering and recognizing, from the outward responses, we try to become conscious of the inner recesses, of the deeper motives and urges; we probe deeper and deeper into the vast depths of the mind. This whole process of challenges and responses, of the movement of experiencing and recognizing the hidden and the open activities, this whole is consciousness bound to time.

The cup is not only the shape, the colour, the design but also that emptiness inside the cup. The cup is the emptiness held within a form; without that emptiness there would be no cup nor form. We know consciousness by outer signs, by its limitations of height and depth, of thought and feeling. But all this is the outer form of consciousness; from the outer we try to find the inner. Is this possible? Theories and speculations are not significant; they actually prevent all discovery. From the outer we try to find the inner, from the known we probe hoping to find the unknown. Is it possible to probe from the inner to the outer? The instrument that probes from the outer we know, but is there such an instrument that probes from the unknown to the known? Is there? And how can there be? There cannot be. If there is one, it's recognizable and if it's recognizable, it's within the area of the known.

That strange benediction comes when it will, but with each visitation, deep within, there is a transformation; it is never the same.

21 August 1961

Again, it has been a clear, sunny day, with long shadows and sparkling leaves; the mountains were serene, solid, and close;

the sky was of an extraordinary blue, spotless and gentle. Shadows filled the earth; it was a morning for shadows, the little ones and the big ones, the long, lean ones and the fat satisfied ones, the squat homely ones and the joyful, spritely ones. The roof-tops of the farms and the chalets shone like polished marble, the new and the old. There seemed to be a great rejoicing and shouting among the trees and meadows; they existed for each other and above them was heaven, not the man-made, with its tortures and hopes. And there was life, vast, splendid, throbbing and stretching in all directions. It was life, always young and always dangerous; life that never stayed, that wandered through the earth, indifferent, never leaving a mark, never asking or calling for anything. It was there in abundance, shadowless and deathless; it didn't care from where it came or where it was going. Wherever it was there was life, beyond time and thought. It was a marvellous thing, free, light, and unfathomable. It was not to be closed in; where they closed it, in the places of worship, in the market place, in the home, there was decay and corruption and their perpetual reform. It was there simple, majestic, and shattering and the beauty of it is beyond thought and feeling. It is so vast and incomparable that it fills the earth and heavens and the blade of grass that's destroyed so soon. It is there with love and death.

It was cool in the wood, with a shouting stream a few feet below; the pines shot up to the skies, without ever bending to look at the earth. It was splendid there with black squirrels eating tree mushrooms and chasing each other up and down the trees in narrow spirals; there was a robin that bobbed up and down, or what looked like a robin. It was cool and quiet there, except for the stream with its cold mountain waters. And there it was, love, creation and destruction, not as a symbol, not in thought and feeling but an actual reality. You couldn't see it, feel it, but it was there, shatteringly immense, strong as ten thousand and with the power of the most vulnerable. It was there and all things became still, the brain and the body; it was a benediction and the mind was of it.

There is no end to depth; the essence of it is without time and space. It's not to be experienced; experience is such a tawdry thing, so easily got and so easily gone; thought cannot put it together nor can feeling make its way to it. These are silly and immature things. Maturity is not of time, a matter of age, nor does it come through influence and environment. It's not to be bought, neither the books nor the teachers and saviours, the one or the many, can ever create the right climate for this maturity. Maturity is not an end in itself; it comes into being without thought cultivating it, darkly, without meditation, unknowingly. There must be maturity, that ripening in life; not the ripeness that is bred out of disease and turmoil, sorrow and hope. Despair and labour cannot bring this total maturity but it must be there, unsought.

For in this total maturity there is austerity. Not the austerity of ashes and sackcloth but that casual and unpremeditated indifference to the things of the world, its virtues, its gods, its respectability, its hopes and values. These must be totally denied for that austerity that comes with aloneness. No influence of society or of culture can ever touch this aloneness. But it must be there, not conjured up by the brain, which is the child of time and influence. It must come thunderingly out of nowhere. And without it, there's no total maturity. Loneliness—the essence of self-pity and self-defence and life in isolation, in myth, in knowledge and idea—is far away from aloneness; in them there is everlasting attempt to integrate and ever breaking apart. Aloneness is a life in which all influence has come to an end. It's this aloneness that is the essence of austerity.

22 August 1961

In the air there was that feeling of unbearable immensity, intense and insistent. It was not a fanciful imagination; imagination ceases when there's reality; imagination is dangerous; it has no validity, only fact has. Fancy and imagination are pleasurable and deceptive and they must be wholly banished. Every form of myth, fancy, and imagination must be understood and this very understanding deprives them of their significance. It was there, and what was started as meditation, ended. Of what significance is meditation when reality is there! It was not meditation that brought reality into being, nothing can bring it into being; it was there in spite of meditation, but what was necessary was a very sensitive, alert brain that had stopped entirely, willingly, and easily, its chatter of reason and non-reason. It had become very quiet, seeing and listening without interpreting, without classifying; it was quiet and there was no entity or necessity to make it quiet. The brain was very still and very alive. That immensity filled the night and there was bliss.

It had no relationship with anything; it was not trying to shape, to change, to assert; it had no influence and therefore was implacable. It was not doing good, not reforming; it was not becoming respectable and so highly destructive. But it was love, not the love that society cultivates, a tortured thing. It was the essence of the movement of life. It was there, implacable, destructive, with a tenderness that the new alone knows, as the new leaf of spring, and it will tell you. And there was strength beyond measure and there was power that only creation has. And all things were quiet. That one star that was going over the hill was now high up and it was bright in its solitude.

New Delhi, 31 October 1956

Questioner: How can I experience God, which will give a meaning to my weary life? Without that experience what is the purpose of living?

Krishnamurti: Can I understand life directly, or must I experience something that will give a meaning to life? Do you understand, sirs? To appreciate beauty, must I know what its purpose is? Must love have a cause? And if there is a cause to love, is it love? The questioner says he must have a certain experience that will give a meaning to life—which implies that for him life in itself is not important. So in seeking God he is really escaping from life, escaping from sorrow, from beauty, from ugliness, from anger, pettiness, jealousy, and the desire for power, from the extraordinary complexity of living. All that is life, and as he does not understand it, he says, 'I will find some greater thing that will give a meaning to life.'

Please listen to what I am saying, but not just at the verbal, intellectual level because then it will have very little meaning. You can spin a lot of words about all this, read all the sacred books in the land, but it will be worthless because it is not related to your life, to your daily existence.

What is our living? What is this thing that we call our existence? Very simply, not philosophically, it is a series of experiences of pleasure and pain, and we want to avoid the pains while holding on to the pleasures. The pleasure of power, of being a big man in the big world, the pleasure of dominating one's little wife or husband, the pain, the frustration, fear, and anxiety that come with ambition, the ugliness of playing up to the man of importance, and so on—all that goes to make up our daily living. That is, what we call living is a series of memories within the field of the known; and the known becomes a problem when the mind is not free of the known. Functioning within the field of the known—the known being knowledge, experience, and the memory of that experience—the mind says, 'I must know God.' So according to its tradition, according to its ideas, its conditioning, it projects an entity that it calls 'God'; but that entity is the result of the known; it is still within the field of time.

So you can find out with clarity, with truth, with real experience whether there is God or not, only when the mind is totally free from the known. Surely that something, which may be called God or truth, must be totally new, unrecognizable, and a mind that approaches it through knowledge, through experience, through ideas and accumulated virtues, is trying to capture the unknown while living in the field of the known, which is an impossibility. All that the mind can do is to inquire into whether it is possible to free itself from the known. To be free from the known is to be completely free from all the impressions of the past, from the whole weight of tradition. The mind itself is the product of the known, it is put together by time as the 'me' and the 'not-me', which is the conflict of duality. If the known totally ceases, consciously as well as unconsciously—and I say, not theoretically, that there is a possibility of its ceasing—then you will never ask if there is God, because such a mind is immeasurable in itself. Like love, it is its own eternity.

Ojai, 5 July 1953

K<small>NOWING THE WHOLE</small> content of the mind—its denials, its resistances, its disciplinary activities, its various efforts at security, all of which condition and limit its thinking—can the mind, as an integrated process, be totally free to discover that which is eternal? Because without that discovery, without the experiencing of that reality, all our problems with their solutions only lead to further misery and disaster. That is obvious, you can see it in everyday life. Individually, politically, internationally, in every activity, we are breeding more and more mischief, which is inevitable as long as we have not experienced that state of religion, that state that is experienceable only when the mind is totally free.

After hearing this, can you, if only for a second, know that freedom? You cannot know it merely because I am suggesting it, for then it would be only an idea, an opinion without any significance. But if you have followed very seriously, you are beginning to be aware of the process of your own thought, of its direction, its purposes, its motives; and being aware, you are bound to come to a state in which the mind is no longer seeking, choosing, struggling to achieve. Having perceived its own total process, the mind becomes extraordinarily still, without any direction, without any volition, without any action of will. Will is still desire, is it not? The man who is ambitious in the worldly sense has a strong desire to achieve, to be successful, to become famous, and he exercises will for his self-importance. Likewise, we exercise will to develop virtue, to achieve a so-called spiritual state. But what I am talking about is totally different; it is devoid entirely of any desire, of any action towards escape, of any compulsion to be this or that.

In examining what I am saying, you are exercising reason, are you not? But reason can lead only so far and no further. We must obviously exercise reason, the capacity to think things out completely and not stop half way. But when reason has reached its limit and can go no further, then the mind is no longer the instrument of reason, of cunning, of calculation, of attack and defence, because the very centre from which arise all our thoughts, all our conflicts, has come to an end.

So now that you have listened, surely you are beginning to be aware of yourself from moment to moment during the day in your various activities. The mind is coming to know itself, with all its deviations, its resistances, its beliefs, its pursuits, its ambitions, its fears, its urge to fulfil. Being aware of all this, is it not possible for the mind, if only for an instant, to be totally still, to know a silence in which there is freedom? And when there is that freedom of silence, then is not the mind itself the eternal?

To experience the unknown, the mind itself must be the unknown. The mind, so far, is the result of the known. What are you but the accumulation of the known, of all your troubles, your vanities, your ambitions, pains, fulfilments, and frustrations? All that is the known, the known in time and space; and as long as the mind is functioning within the field of time, of the known, it can never be the unknown, it can only go on experiencing that which it has known. Please, this is not something complicated or mysterious. I am describing obvious facts of our daily existence. Burdened with the known, the mind seeks to discover the unknown. How can it? We all talk of God: In every religion, in every church and temple that word is used, but always in the image of the known. It is only the very, very few who leave all the churches, the temples, the books, who go beyond and discover.

At present, the mind is the result of time, of the known, and when such a mind sets out to discover, it can discover only what it has already experienced, which is the known. To discover the unknown, the mind has to free itself completely from the known, from the past, not by slow analysis, not by delving step by step into the past, interpreting every dream, every reaction, but by seeing the truth of all this completely, instantaneously, as you are sitting there. As long as the mind is the result of time, of the known, it can never find the unknown, which is God, reality, or what you will. Seeing the truth of that frees the mind from the past. Don't immediately translate freedom from the past as not knowing the way to your home. That is amnesia. Don't reduce it to such infantile thinking. But the mind is freed the moment it sees the truth that it cannot find the real, this extraordinary state of the unknown, when it is burdened with the known. Knowledge, experience is the 'me', the ego, the self that has accumulated, gathered; therefore all knowledge must be suspended, all experience must be set aside. And when there is the silence of freedom, then is not the mind itself the eternal? Then it is experiencing something totally new, which is the real; but to experience that, the mind must be that. Please don't say the mind is reality. It is not. The mind can experience reality only when it is totally free from time.

This whole process of discovery is religion. Surely religion is not what you believe; it has nothing to do with whether you are a Christian or a Buddhist, a Moslem, or a Hindu. Those things have no significance; they are a hindrance, and the mind that would discover must be totally stripped of them all. To be new, the mind must be alone. For eternal creation to be, the mind itself must be in that state to receive it. But as long as it is full of its own travails and struggles, as long as it is burdened with knowledge and complicated by psychological blockages, the mind can never be free to receive, to understand, to discover.

A truly religious person is not one who is encrusted with beliefs, dogmas, rituals. He has no beliefs; he is living from moment to moment, never accumulating any experience, and therefore he is the only revolutionary being. Truth is not a continuity in time; it must be discovered anew at every moment. The mind that gathers, holds, that treasures any experience, cannot live from moment to moment discovering the new.

Those who are really serious, who are not dilettantes, not merely playing with all this, have an extraordinary importance in life, because it is they who will become a light unto themselves and therefore, perhaps, to others. To talk of God without experiencing, without having a mind that is totally free and thereby open to the unknown, has very little value. It is like grown-up people playing with toys; and when we play with toys, calling it 'religion', we are creating more confusion, greater misery.

It is only when we understand the whole process of thinking, when we are no longer caught in our own thought, that it is possible for the mind to be still. And only then can the eternal come into being.

Ojai, 21 August 1955, Talk

Iᴛ ɪs ᴀɴ obvious fact that human beings demand something to worship. You and I and many others desire to have something sacred in our lives, and either we go to temples, to mosques, or to churches, or we have other symbols, images, and ideas that we worship. The necessity to worship something seems very urgent because we want to be taken out of ourselves into something greater, wider, more profound, more permanent. So we begin to invent masters, teachers, divine beings in heaven or on the earth; we devise various symbols, the cross, the crescent, and so on. If none of that is satisfactory, we speculate about what lies beyond the mind, holding that it is something sacred, something to be worshipped. That is what happens in our everyday existence, as I think most of us are well aware. There is always this effort within the field of the known, within the field of the mind, of memory, and we never seem able to break away and find something sacred that is not manufactured by the mind.

I would like, if I may, to go into this question of whether there is something really sacred, something immeasurable that cannot be fathomed by the mind. To do that, there must obviously be a revolution in our thinking, in our values. I do not mean an economic or social revolution, which is merely immature; it may superficially affect our lives, but fundamentally it is not a revolution at all. I am talking of the revolution that is brought about through self-knowledge, not through the superficial self-knowledge that is achieved by an examination of thought on the surface of the mind, but through the profound depths of self-knowledge.

Surely, one of our greatest difficulties is this fact that all our effort is within the field of recognition. We seem to function only within the limits of that which we are capable of recognizing, that is, within the field of memory; is it possible for the mind to go beyond that field?

Please, if I may suggest, observe your own mind as I am talking; because I want to go into this rather deeply, and if you merely follow the verbal explanation without applying it immediately, the explanation will have no significance whatsoever. If you listen and say, 'I will think about it tomorrow', then it is gone, it has no value at all; but if you give complete attention to what is being said and are capable of applying it, which means being aware of your own intellectual and emotional processes, then you will see that what I am saying has significance immediately.

❖

You see, we think we understand things by accumulating knowledge, by comparing. Surely we do not understand in that way. If you compare one thing with another, you are merely lost in comparison. You can understand something only when you give it your complete attention, and any form of comparison or evaluation is a distraction.

Self-knowledge, then, is not cumulative, and I think it is very important to understand that. If self-knowledge is cumulative, it is merely mechanical. It is like the knowledge of a doctor who has learned a technique and everlastingly specializes in a certain part of the body. A surgeon may be an excellent mechanic in his surgery because he has learned the technique, he has the knowledge and the gift for it, and there is the cumulative experience that helps him. But we are not talking of such cumulative experience. On the contrary, any form of cumulative knowledge destroys further discovery; but when one discovers, then perhaps one can use the cumulative technique.

Surely what I am saying is quite simple. If one is capable of studying, watching oneself, one begins to discover how cumulative memory is acting on everything one sees; one is forever evaluating, discarding or accepting, condemning or justifying, so one's experience is always within the field of the known, of the conditioned. But without cumulative memory as a directive, most of us feel lost, we feel frightened, and so we are incapable of observing ourselves as we are. When there is the accumulative process, which is the cultivation of memory, our observation of ourselves becomes very superficial. Memory is helpful in directing, improving oneself, but in self-improvement there can never be a revolution, a radical transformation. It is only when the sense of self-improvement completely ceases, but not by volition, that there is a possibility of something transcendental, something totally new coming into being.

❖

IF SOMEONE POINTS out the futility of repeating what others say, of depending on the evidence of others, which may be nonsense, then you must surely say, 'I do not know.' Now, if one can really come to that state of saying, 'I do not know', it indicates an extraordinary sense of humility; there is no arrogance of knowledge, there is no self-assertive answer to make an impression. When you can actually say, 'I do not know', which very few are capable of saying, then in that state all fear ceases, because all sense of recognition, the search into memory, has come to an end; there is no longer inquiry into the field of the known. Then comes the extraordinary thing. If you have so far followed what I am talking about, not just verbally, but if you are actually experiencing it, you will find that when you can say, 'I do not know', all conditioning has stopped. And what then is the state of the mind? Do you understand what I am talking about? Am I making myself clear? I think it is important for you to give a little attention to this, if you care to.

You see, we are seeking something permanent, permanent in the sense of time, something enduring, everlasting. We see that everything about us is transient, in flux—being born, withering and dying—and our search is always to establish something that will endure within the field of the known. But that which is truly sacred is beyond the measure of time, it is not to be found within the field of the known. The known operates only through thought, which is the response of memory to challenge. If I see that and I want to find out how to end thinking, what am I to do? Surely I must through self-knowledge be aware of the whole process of my thinking. I must see that every thought, however subtle, however lofty, or however ignoble, stupid, has its roots in the known, in memory. If I see that very clearly, then the mind, when confronted with an immense problem, is capable of saying, 'I do not know', because it has no answer. Then all the answers—of the Buddha, of the Christ, of the masters, the teachers, the gurus—have no meaning; because if they have a meaning, that meaning is born of the collection of memories that is my conditioning.

If I see the truth of all that and actually put aside all the answers, which I can do only when there is this immense humility of not-knowing, then what is the state of the mind? What is the state of the mind that says, 'I do not know whether there is God, whether there is love'—that is, when there is no response of memory? Please don't immediately answer the question to yourselves because if you do, your answer will be merely the recognition of what you think it should or should not be. If you say, 'It is a state of negation', you are comparing it with something that you already know; therefore that state in which you say, 'I do not know', is non-existent.

I am trying to inquire into this problem aloud so that you also can follow it through the observation of your own mind. That state in which the mind says, 'I do not know', is not negation. The mind has completely stopped searching, it has ceased making any movement, for it sees that any movement out of the known towards the thing it calls the unknown is only a projection of the known. The mind that is capable of saying, 'I do not know', is in the only state in which anything can be discovered. But the man who says, 'I know', the man who has studied infinitely the varieties of human experience and whose mind is burdened with information, with encyclopaedic knowledge, can he ever experience something that is not to be accumulated? He will find it extremely hard. When the mind totally puts aside all the knowledge that it has acquired, when for it there are no Buddhas, no Christs, no masters, no teachers, no religions, no quotations, when the mind is completely alone, un-contaminated—which means that the movement of the known has come to an end—it is only then that there is a possibility of a tremendous revolution, a fundamental change. Such a change is obviously necessary; and it is only the few, you and I, or X, who have brought about in themselves this revolution, who are capable of creating a new world, not the idealists, not the intellectuals, not the people who have immense knowledge, or who are doing good works. They are not the people; they are all reformers. The religious man is he who does not belong to any religion, to any nation, to any race, who is inwardly completely alone, in a state of not-knowing. And for him the blessing of the sacred comes into being.

Ojai, 21 August 1955, Questions

Questioner: The function of the mind is to think. I have spent a great many years thinking about the things we all know—business, science, philosophy, psychology, the arts, and so on—and now I think a great deal about God. From studying the evidence of many mystics and other religious writers, I am convinced that God exists, and I am able to contribute my own thoughts on the subject. What is wrong with this? Does not thinking about God help to bring about the realization of God?

Krishnamurti: Can you think about God? Can you be convinced about the existence of God because you have read all the evidence? The atheist also has his evidence; he has probably studied as much as you, and he says there is no God. You believe that there is God, and he believes that there is not; both of you have beliefs, both of you spend your time thinking about God. But before you think about something that you do not know, you must find out what thinking is, must you not? How can you think about something that you do not know? You may have read the Bible, the Bhagavad Gita, or other books in which various erudite scholars have skilfully described what God is, asserting this and contradicting that, but as long as you do not know the process of your own thinking, what you think about God may be stupid and petty, and generally it is. You may collect a lot of evidence for the existence of God and write very clever articles about it, but surely the first question is, how do you know what you think is true? Can thinking ever bring about the experience of that which is unknowable? Which doesn't mean that you must emotionally, sentimentally *accept* some rubbish about God.

So is it not important to find out whether your mind is conditioned, rather than to seek that which is unconditioned? Surely if your mind is conditioned, which it is, however much it may inquire into the reality of God, it can only gather knowledge or information according to its conditioning. So your thinking about God is an utter waste of time, it is a speculation that has no value. It is like my sitting in this grove and wishing to be on the top of that mountain [in the background]. If I really want to find out what is on the top of the mountain and beyond, I must go to it. It is no good my sitting here speculating, building temples, churches, and getting excited about them. What I have to do is to stand up, walk, struggle, push, get there, and find out; but as most of us are unwilling to do that, we are satisfied to sit here and speculate about something that we do not know. And I say such speculation is a hindrance, it is a deterioration of the mind, it has no value at all; it only brings more confusion, more sorrow to man.

God is something that cannot be talked about, that cannot be described, that cannot be put into words, because it must ever remain the unknown. The moment the recognizing process takes place, you are back in the field of memory. Do you understand? Say, for instance, you have a momentary experience of something extraordinary. At that precise moment there is no thinker who says, 'I must remember it.' There is only the state of experiencing. But when that moment goes by, the process of recognition comes into being. Please follow this. The mind says, 'I have had a marvellous experience and I wish I could have more of it', so the struggle for the more begins. The acquisitive instinct, the possessive pursuit of the more, comes into being for various reasons: because it gives you pleasure, prestige, knowledge, you become an authority, and all the rest of that nonsense.

The mind pursues that which it has experienced, but that which it has experienced is already over, dead, gone. To discover that which is, the mind must die to that which it has experienced. This is not something that can be cultivated day after day, that can be gathered, accumulated, held, and then talked and written about. All that we can do is to see that the mind is conditioned and through self-knowledge to understand the process of our own thinking. I must know myself, not as I would ideologically like to be, but as I actually am, however ugly or beautiful, however jealous, envious, acquisitive. But it is very difficult just to see what one is without wishing to change it, and that very desire to change it is another form of conditioning; and so we go on, moving from conditioning to conditioning, never experiencing something beyond that which is limited.

Q: I have listened to you for many years and I have become quite good at watching my own thoughts and being aware of every thing I do, but I have never touched the deep waters or experienced the transformation of which you speak. Why?

K: I think it is fairly clear why none of us do experience something beyond the mere watching. There may be rare moments of an emotional state in which we see, as it were, the clarity of the sky between clouds, but I do not mean anything of that kind. All such experiences are temporary and have very little significance. The questioner wants to know why, after these many years of watching, he hasn't found the deep waters. Why should he find them? Do you understand? You think that by watching your own thoughts you are going to get a reward; if you do this, you will get that. You are really not watching at all, because your mind is concerned with gaining a reward. You think that by watching, by being aware, you will be more loving, you will suffer less, be less irritable, get something beyond, so your watching is a process of buying. With this coin you are buying that, which means that your watching is a process of choice; therefore it isn't watching, it isn't attention. To watch is to observe without choice, to see yourself as you are without any movement of desire to change, which is an extremely arduous thing to do; but that doesn't mean that you are going to remain in your present state. You do not know what will happen if you see yourself as you are without wishing to bring about a change in that which you see. Do you understand?

I am going to take an example and work it out, and you will see. Let us say I am violent, as most people are. Our whole culture is violent—but I won't enter into the anatomy of violence now because that is not the problem we are considering. I am violent, and I realize that I am violent. What happens? My immediate response is that I must do something about it, is it not? I say I must become non-violent. That is what every religious teacher has told us for centuries: that if one is violent one must become non-violent. So I practise, I do all the ideological things. But now I see how absurd that is because the entity who observes violence, and wishes to change it into non-violence, is still violent. So I am concerned, not with the expression of that entity, but with the entity himself. You are following all this I hope.

Now what is that entity who says, 'I must not be violent'? Is that entity different from the violence he has observed? Are they two different states? Do you understand, sirs, or is this too abstract? Surely the violence and the entity who says, 'I must change violence into non-violence', are both the same. To recognize that fact is to put an end to all conflict, is it not? There is no longer the conflict of trying to change, because I see that the very movement of the mind not to be violent is itself the outcome of violence.

The questioner wants to know why it is that he cannot go beyond all these superficial wrangles of the mind. For the simple reason that, consciously or unconsciously, the mind is always seeking something, and that very search brings violence, competition, the sense of utter dissatisfaction. It is only when the mind is completely still that there is a possibility of touching the deep waters.

Q: When we die, are we reborn on this earth, or do we pass on into some other world?

K: This question interests all of us, the young and the old, does it not? So I am going into it rather deeply, and I hope you will be good enough to follow, not just the words, but the actual experience of what I am going to discuss with you.

We all know that death exists, especially the older people, and also the young who observe it. The young say, 'Wait till it comes and we'll deal with it.' And the old, who are nearer death, have recourse to various forms of consolation.

Please follow and apply this to yourselves, don't put it onto somebody else. Because you know you are going to die; you have theories about it, don't you? You believe in God. You believe in resurrection, or in karma and reincarnation. You say that you will be reborn here, or in another world. Or you rationalize death, saying that death is inevitable, it happens to everybody; the tree withers away, nourishing the soil, and a new tree comes up. Or else you are too occupied with your daily worries, anxieties, jealousies, envies, with your competition and your wealth, to think about death at all. But it is in your mind; consciously or unconsciously it is there.

First of all, can you be free of the beliefs, the rationalities, or the indifference that you have cultivated towards death? Can you be free of all that now? Because what is important is to enter the house of death while living, while fully conscious, active, in health, and not wait for the coming of death, which may carry you off instantaneously through an accident, or through a disease that slowly makes you unconscious. When death comes it must be an extraordinary moment that is as vital as living.

Now, can I, can you, enter the house of death while living? That is the problem, not whether there is reincarnation, or whether there is another world where you will be reborn, which is all so immature, so infantile. A man who lives never asks what is living and he has no theories about living. It is only the half-alive who talk about the purpose of life.

So can you and I, while living, conscious, active, with all our capacities whatever they be, know what death is? And is death then different from living? To most of us, living is a continuation of that which we think is permanent. Our name, our family, our property, the things in which we have a vested interest economically and spiritually, the virtues that we have cultivated, the things that we have acquired emotionally; all of that we want to continue. And the moment that we call death is a moment of the unknown. Therefore we are frightened, so we try to find a consolation, some kind of comfort; we want to know if there is life after death, and a dozen other things. Those are all irrelevant problems; they are problems for the lazy, for those who do not want to find out what death is while living. So can you and I find out?

What is death? Surely it is the complete cessation of everything that you have known. If it is not the cessation of everything you have known, it is not death. If you know death already then you have nothing to be frightened of. But do you know death? That is, can you while living put an end to this everlasting struggle to find in the impermanent something that will continue? Can you know the unknowable, that state that we call death, while living? Can you put aside all the descriptions of what happens after death that you have read in books, or that your unconscious desire for comfort dictates, and taste or experience that state—which must be extraordinary—now? If that state can be experienced now, then living and dying are the same.

So can I, who have vast education, knowledge, who have had innumerable experiences, struggles, loves, hates, can that 'I' come to an end? The 'I' is the recorded memory of all that; and can that 'I' come to an end? Without being brought to an end by an accident, by a disease, can you and I while sitting here know that end? Then you will find that you will no longer ask foolish questions about death and continuity, or whether there is a world hereafter.

Then you will know the answer for yourself because that which is unknowable will have come into being. Then you will put aside the whole rigmarole of reincarnation, and the many fears—the fear of living and the fear of dying, the fear of growing old and inflicting on others the trouble of looking after you, the fear of loneliness and dependency—will all have come to an end. These are not vain words. It is only when the mind ceases to think in terms of its own continuity that the unknowable comes into being.

Saanen, 2 August 1964

I WOULD LIKE to talk over, not merely to explain verbally, but also to understand deeply, the significance of religion. But before we can penetrate deeply into this question, we shall have to be very clear as to what is the religious mind, and what is the state of a mind that really inquires into the whole question of religion.

It seems to me very important to understand the difference between isolation and aloneness. Most of our daily activity is centred around ourselves; it is based on our particular point of view, on our particular experiences and idiosyncrasies. We think in terms of our family, of our job, of what we wish to achieve, and also in terms of our fears, hopes, and despairs. All this is obviously self-centred and it brings about a state of self-isolation, as we can see in our daily life. We have our own secret desires, our hidden pursuits and ambitions, and we are never deeply related to anyone, either to our wives, our husbands, or our children. This self-isolation is likewise the result of our running away from our daily boredom, from the frustrations and trivialities of our daily life. It is caused also by our escaping in various ways from the extraordinary sense of loneliness that comes over us when we suddenly feel unrelated to anything, when everything is in the distance and there is no communion, no relationship with anyone. I think most of us, if we are at all aware of the process of our own being, have felt this loneliness very deeply.

Because of this loneliness, out of this sense of isolation, we try to identify ourselves with something greater than the mind—it may be the State, or an ideal, or a concept of what God is. This identification with something great or immortal, something outside the field of our own thought, is generally called religion, and it leads to belief, dogma, ritual, the separative pursuits of competing groups, each believing in different aspects of the same thing. So what we call religion brings about still further isolation.

Then one sees how the earth is divided into competing nations, each with its sovereign government and economic barriers. Though we are all human beings, we have built walls between ourselves and our neighbours through nationalism, through race, caste, and class, which again breeds isolation, loneliness.

Now a mind that is caught in loneliness, in this state of isolation, can never possibly understand what religion is. It can believe, it can have certain theories, concepts, formulas, it can try to identify itself with that which it calls God, but religion, it seems to me, has nothing whatsoever to do with any belief, with any priest, with any church, or so-called sacred book. The state of the religious mind can be understood only when we begin to understand what beauty is, and the understanding of beauty must be approached through total aloneness. Only when the mind is completely alone can it know what beauty is, and not in any other state.

Aloneness is obviously not isolation, and it is not uniqueness. To be unique is merely to be exceptional in some way, whereas to be completely alone demands extraordinary sensitivity, intelligence, understanding. To be completely alone implies that the mind is free of every kind of influence, and is therefore uncontaminated by society. And it must be alone to understand what religion is—which is to find out for oneself whether there is something immortal, beyond time.

As it is now, the mind is the result of many thousands of years of influence—biological, sociological, environmental, climatic, alimentary, and so on. This is fairly obvious. You are influenced by the food you eat, by the newspapers you read, by your wife or husband, by your neighbour, by the politician, by radio and television, and a thousand other things. You are constantly being influenced by what is poured into the conscious as well as into the unconscious mind from many different directions. Is it not possible to be so aware of these many influences that one is not caught in any of them and remains totally uncontaminated by them? Otherwise the mind merely becomes an instrument of its environment. It may create an image of what it thinks is God, or the Eternal Truth, and believe in that, but it is still shaped by environmental demands, tensions, superstitions, pressures, and its belief is not the state of a religious mind at all.

As a Christian you were brought up in a church built by man over a period of two thousand years, with its priests, dogmas, rituals. In childhood you were baptized, and as you grew up you were told what to believe; you went through that whole process of conditioning, brainwashing. The pressure of this propagandist religion is obviously very strong, particularly because it is well organized and able to exert psychological influence through education, through the worship of images, through fear, able to condition the mind in a thousand other ways. Throughout the East people are also heavily conditioned by their beliefs, their dogmas, their superstitions, and by a tradition that goes back ten thousand years or more.

Now unless the mind has freedom, it cannot find out what is true, and to have freedom is to be free from influence. You have to be free from the influence of your nationality and from the influence of your church, with its beliefs and dogmas, and you also have to be free of greed, envy, fear, sorrow, ambition, competition, anxiety. If the mind is not free from all these things, the various pressures from outside and within itself will create a contradictory, neurotic state, and such a mind cannot possibly discover what is true, or if there is something beyond time.

So one sees how necessary it is for the mind to be free from all influence. Is such a thing possible? If it is not possible, then there can be no discovery of what is the eternal, the unnameable, the supreme. To find out for oneself whether it is possible or not, one has to be aware of these many influences, not only sitting here, but also in one's daily life. One has to observe how they are contaminating, shaping, conditioning the mind. One obviously cannot be aware all the time of the many different influences that are pouring in on the mind, but one can see the importance—and I think this is the crux of the matter—of being free of all influence. When once one understands the necessity of that, then the unconscious is aware of influence even though the conscious mind may often not be.

Am I making myself clear? What I am trying to point out is this: There are extraordinarily subtle influences that are shaping your mind, and a mind that is shaped by influences that are always within the field of time, cannot possibly discover the eternal, or if there is such a thing as the eternal. So the question then is: If the conscious mind cannot possibly be aware of all the many influences, what is it to do? If you put this question to yourself very seriously and earnestly so that it demands your complete attention, you will find that the unconscious part of you that is not totally occupied when the upper layers of the mind are functioning, takes charge and watches all the influences that are coming in.

I think this is very important to understand, because if you merely resist, or defend yourself against being influenced, that resistance, which is a reaction, creates a further conditioning of the mind. The understanding of the total process of influence must be effortless; it must have the quality of immediate perception. It is like this: If you really see for yourself the tremendous importance of not being influenced, then a certain part of your mind takes charge of the matter whenever you are consciously occupied with other things, and that part of the mind is very alert, active, watchful. So what is important is to see immediately the enormous significance of not being influenced by any circumstances or by any person whatsoever. That is the real point, not how to resist influence, or what to do in case you are influenced. Once you have grasped this central fact, then you will find there is a part of the mind that is always alert and watching, always ready to cleanse itself of every influence,

however subtle. Out of this freedom from all influence comes aloneness, which is entirely different from isolation. And there must be
aloneness, because beauty is outside the field of time, and only the
mind that is completely alone can know what beauty is.

For most of us, beauty is a matter of proportion, shape, size,
contour, colour. We see a building, a tree, a mountain, a river, and we
say it is beautiful; but there is still the outsider, the experiencer
who is looking at these things, and therefore what we call beauty is
still within the field of time. But I feel that beauty is beyond time
and that to know beauty there must be the ending of the experiencer. The experiencer is merely an accumulation of experience
from which to judge, to evaluate, to think. When the mind looks at a
picture, or listens to music, or sees the swift flowing of a river, it generally does so from that background of accumulated experience; it
is looking from the past, from the field of time, and to me that is
not to know beauty at all. To know beauty, which is to find out
what is the eternal, is possible only when the mind is completely
alone. And that has nothing whatsoever to do with what the priests
say, with what the organized religions say. The mind must be totally
uninfluenced, uncontaminated by society, by the psychological
structure of greed, envy, anxiety, fear. It must be completely free
of all that. Out of this freedom comes aloneness, and it is only in
the state of aloneness that the mind can know that which is beyond
the field of time.

Beauty and that which is eternal cannot be separated. You
may paint, you may write, you may observe nature, but if there is the
activity of the self in any form, any self-centred movement of
thought, then what you perceive ceases to be beauty, because it is
still within the field of time. And if you don't understand beauty,
you cannot possibly find out what is the eternal, because the two
go together. To find out what is the eternal, the immortal, your mind
must be free of time—time being tradition, the accumulated knowledge and experience of the past. It is not a question of what you
believe or disbelieve; that is immature, utterly juvenile, and it has

absolutely nothing to do with the matter. But the mind that is in earnest, that really wants to find out, will relinquish totally the self-centred activity of isolation, and will thereby come upon a state in which it is completely alone. It is only in that state of complete aloneness that there can be the comprehension of beauty, of that which is eternal.

You know, words are dangerous things because they are symbols, and symbols are not the real. They convey a significance, a concept, but the word is not the thing. So when I am talking about the eternal, you have to find out if you are merely being influenced by my words or are caught up in a belief, which would be too infantile.

Now to find out if there is such a thing as the eternal, one has to understand what time is. Time is a most extraordinary thing. I am not talking about chronological time, time by the watch, which is both obvious and necessary. I am talking about time as psychological continuity. Is it possible to live without that continuity? What gives continuity, surely, is thought. If one thinks about something constantly, it has a continuity. If one looks at a picture of one's wife every day, one gives it a continuity. Is it possible to live in this world without giving continuity to action, so that one comes to every action afresh? That is, can I die to each action throughout the day, so that the mind never accumulates and is therefore never contaminated by the past, but is always new, fresh, innocent? I say that such a thing is possible, that one can live in this way. But that does not mean it is real for you. You have to find out for yourself.

So one begins to see that the mind must be completely alone, but not isolated. In this state of complete aloneness there comes a sense of extraordinary beauty, of something not created by the mind. It has nothing to do with putting a few notes together, or using a few paints to create a picture, but because it is alone the mind is in beauty, and therefore it is completely sensitive. And being completely sensitive, it is intelligent. Its intelligence is not the intelligence of cunning or knowledge, nor is it the capacity to do something. The mind is intelligent in the sense that it is not being dominated, influenced and is unafraid. But to be in that state the mind must be able to renew itself every day, which is to die every day to the past, to everything it has known.

As I said, the word, the symbol, is not the real. The word *tree* is not the tree, and so one has to be very alert not to be caught in words. When the mind is free of the word, the symbol, it becomes astonishingly sensitive, and then it is in a state of finding out.

After all, man has been seeking this thing for so long, from very ancient times until now. He wants to find something that is not man-made. Though organized religion has no meaning for any intelligent man, nevertheless the organized religions have always said that there is something beyond. Man has always sought that something, because he is everlastingly in sorrow, in misery, in confusion, in despair. Being always in a state of transiency, he wants to find something permanent, something that will last, endure, that will have a continuity, and therefore his seeking has always been within the field of time. But as one can observe, there is nothing permanent. Our relationships, our jobs, everything is impermanent. Because of our tremendous fear of this impermanence, we are always seeking something permanent that we call the immortal, the eternal, or what you will. But this search for the permanent, the immortal, the eternal is merely a reaction, and therefore it is not valid. It is only when the mind is free of this desire to be certain that it can begin to find out if there is such a thing as the eternal, something beyond space, beyond time, beyond the thinker and the thing that he is thinking about or seeking. To observe and understand all this requires total attention, and the pliable quality of discipline that comes out of that attention. In such attention there is no distraction, there is no strain, there is no movement in any particular direction, because every such movement, every motive, is the result of influence, either of the past or of the present. In that state of effortless attention there comes an extraordinary sense of freedom, and only then, being totally empty, quiet, still, is the mind capable of discovering that which is eternal.

Perhaps you wish to ask questions about what has been said.

Questioner: How is one to be free from the desire to be certain?

Krishnamurti: The word *how* implies a method, does it not? If you are a builder and I ask you how to build a house, you can tell me what to do, because there is a method, a system, a way to set about it. But the following of a method or a system has already conditioned the mind, so just see the difficulty in the use of that word *how*.

Then we also have to understand desire. . . . What is desire? There is seeing or perception, then contact or touching, then sensation, and finally the arising of that which we call desire. Surely this is what takes place. Please follow it closely. There is the seeing, let us say, of a beautiful car. From that very act of seeing, even without touching the car, there is sensation, which creates the desire to drive it, to own it. We are not concerned with how to resist or be free of desire, because the man who has resisted and thinks he is free of desire is really paralysed, dead. What is important is to understand the whole process of desire, which is to know both its importance and its total unimportance. One has to find out, not how to end desire, but what it is that gives continuity to desire.

Now what gives continuity to desire? It is thought, is it not? First there is the seeing of the car, then the sensation, which is followed by the desire. And if thought does not interfere and give continuity to the desire by saying, 'I must have that car, how shall I get it?' then the desire comes to an end. Do you follow? I am not insisting that there should be freedom from desire; on the contrary. But you must understand the whole structure of desire, and then you will find there is no longer a continuity of desire, but something else altogether.

So what is important is not desire, but the fact that we give it continuity. For instance, we give sexuality a continuity through thought, through images, through pictures, through sensation, through remembrance; we keep the memory going by thinking about it, and all this gives continuity to sexuality, to the importance of the senses. Not that the senses are not important, they are. But we give the pleasure of the senses a continuity that becomes overwhelmingly important in our life. So what matters is not freedom from desire, but to understand the structure of desire and how thought gives it continuity—and that is all. Then the mind is free, and you do not have to seek freedom from desire. The moment you seek freedom from desire, you are caught in conflict. Each time you see a car, a woman, a house, or whatever it may be that attracts you, thought steps in and gives desire a continuity, and then it all becomes an endless problem.

What is important is to live a life without effort, without a single problem. You can live without a problem if you understand the nature of effort and see very clearly the whole structure of desire. Most of us have a thousand problems, and to be free of problems we must be able to end each problem immediately as it arises. It is absolutely necessary for the mind to have no problems at all, and so live a life without effort. Surely such a mind is the only religious mind, because it has understood sorrow and the ending of sorrow. It is without fear, and is therefore a light unto itself.

Saanen, 1 August 1965

PLEASE, AS I said the other day, the speaker is not important; what he says is important, because what he says is the voice of your own self talking aloud. Through the words that the speaker is using, you are listening to yourself, not to the speaker, and therefore listening becomes extraordinarily important. To listen is to learn, and not to accumulate. If you accumulate knowledge and listen from that accumulation, from your background of knowledge, then you are not listening. It is only when you listen that you learn. You are learning about yourself, and therefore you have to listen with care, with extraordinary attention, and attention is denied when you justify, condemn, or otherwise evaluate what you hear. Then you are not listening, you are not perceiving, seeing.

If you sit on the bank of a river after a storm, you see the stream going by carrying a great deal of debris. Similarly, you have to watch the movement of yourself, following every thought, every feeling, every intention, every motive. Just watch it; that watching is also listening. It is being aware with your eyes, with your ears, with your insight, of all the values that human beings have created, and by which you are conditioned. It is only this state of total awareness that will end all seeking.

As I said, seeking and finding is a waste of energy. When the mind itself is unclear, confused, frightened, miserable, anxious, what is the good of its seeking? Out of this chaos, what can you find except more chaos? But when there is inward clarity, when the mind is not frightened, not demanding reassurance, then there is no seeking and therefore no finding. To see God, truth, is not a religious act. The only religious act is to come upon this inward clarity through self-knowing; that is, through being aware of all one's intimate, secret desires and allowing them to unfold, never correcting, controlling, or indulging, but always watching them. Out of that constant watching there comes extraordinary clarity, sensitivity, and a tremendous conservation of energy. And one must have immense energy, because all action is energy, life itself is energy. When we are miserable, anxious, quarrelling, jealous, when we are frightened, when we feel insulted or flattered—all that is a dissipation of energy. It is also a dissipation of energy to be ill, physically or inwardly. Everything that we do, think, and feel is an outpouring of energy. Either we understand the dissipation of energy and therefore out of that understanding there is a natural coming together of all energy, or we spend our lives struggling to bring together various contradictory expressions of energy, hoping from the peripheral to come to the essence.

The essence of religion is sacredness, which has nothing to do with religious organizations, nor with the mind that is caught and conditioned by a belief, a dogma. To such a mind nothing is sacred except the God it has created, or the ritual it has put together, or the various sensations it derives from prayer, from worship, from devotion. But these things are not sacred at all. There is nothing sacred about dogmatism, about ritualism, about sentimentality or emotionalism. Sacredness is the very essence of a mind that is religious, and that is what we are going to discover. We are not concerned with what is supposed to be sacred—the symbol, the word, the person, the picture, a particular experience, which are all juvenile—but with the essence. That demands on the part of each one of us an understanding that comes through watching, or being aware, first of outward things. The mind cannot ride the tide of inward awareness without first being aware of outward behaviour, outward gestures, costumes, shapes, the size and colour of a tree, the appearance of a person, of a house. It is the same tide that goes out and comes in, and unless you know the outward tide, you will never know what the inward tide is.

Please do listen to this. Most of us think that awareness is a mysterious something to be practised, and that we should get together day after day to talk about awareness. You don't come to awareness that way at all. But if you are aware of outward things—the curve of a road, the shape of a tree, the colour of another's clothes, the outline of the mountains against a blue sky, the delicacy of a flower, the pain on the face of a passer-by, the ignorance, the envy, the jealousy of others, the beauty of the earth—then, seeing all these outward things without condemnation, without choice, you can ride on the tide of inner awareness. Then you will become aware of your own reactions, of your own pettiness, of your own jealousies. From the outward awareness, you come to the inward; but if you are not aware of the outer, you cannot possibly come to the inner.

When there is inward awareness of every activity of your mind and your body, when you are aware of your thoughts, of your feelings, both secret and open, conscious and unconscious, then out of this awareness there comes a clarity that is not induced, not put together by the mind. And without that clarity, you may do what you will, you may search the heavens, and the earth, and the deeps, but you will never find out what is true.

So one who would discover what is true must have the sensitivity of awareness, which is not to practise awareness. The practice of awareness only leads to habit, and habit is destructive of all sensitivity. Any habit, whether it is the habit of sex, the habit of drink, the habit of smoking, or what you will, makes the mind insensitive; and a mind that is insensitive, besides dissipating energy, becomes dull. A dull, shallow, conditioned, petty mind may take a drug and for a second it may have an astonishing experience, but it is still a petty mind. What we are now doing is finding out how to put an end to the pettiness of the mind.

Pettiness is not ended by gathering more information, more knowledge, by listening to great music, by seeing the beauty spots of the world, and so on; it has nothing to do with that at all. What brings about the ending of pettiness is the clarity of self-knowing, the movement of the mind that has no restrictions. It is only such a mind that is religious.

The essence of religion is sacredness; but sacredness is not in any church, in any temple, in any mosque, in any image. I am talking about the essence and not about the things that we call sacred. When one understands this essence of religion, which is sacredness, then life has a different meaning altogether; then everything has beauty, and beauty is sacredness. Beauty is not that which stimulates. When you see a mountain, a building, a river, a valley, a flower, or a face, you may say it is beautiful because you are stimulated by it, but the beauty about which I am talking offers no stimulation whatsoever. It is a beauty not to be found in any picture, in any symbol, in any word, in any music. That beauty is sacredness. It is the essence of a religious mind, of a mind that is clear in its self-knowing. One comes upon that beauty, not by desiring, wanting, longing for the experience, but only when all desire for experience has come to an end; and that is one of the most difficult things to understand.

As I pointed out earlier, a mind that is seeking experience is still moving on the periphery, and the translation of each experience will depend on your particular conditioning. Whether you are a Christian, a Buddhist, a Moslem, a Hindu, or a Communist, whatever it is you are, your experiences will obviously be translated and conditioned according to your background, and the more you demand experience, the more you are strengthening that background. This process is not an undoing of, nor a putting an end to, sorrow; it is only an escape from sorrow. A mind that is clear in its self-knowing, a mind that is the very essence of clarity and light, has no need of experience. It is what it is. So clarity comes through self-knowing, and not through the instruction of another, whether he be a clever writer, a psychologist, a philosopher, or a so-called religious teacher.

There is no sacredness without love and the understanding of death. You know, it is one of the most marvellous things in life to discover something unexpectedly, spontaneously, to come upon something without premeditation, and instantly to see the beauty, the sacredness, the reality of it. But a mind that is seeking and wanting to find is never in that position at all. Love is not a thing to be cultivated. Love, like humility, cannot be put together by the mind. It is only the vain man who attempts to be humble; it is only the proud man who seeks to put away his pride through practising humility. The practice of humility is still an act of vanity. To listen and therefore to learn, there must be a spontaneous quality of humility; and a mind that has understood the nature of humility never follows, never obeys. For how can that which is completely negative, empty, obey or follow anyone?

A mind that out of its own clarity of self-knowing has discovered what love is, will also be aware of the nature and the structure of death. If we don't die to the past, to everything of yesterday, then the mind is still caught in its longings, in the shadows of memory, in its conditioning, and so there is no clarity. To die to yesterday easily, voluntarily, without argument or justification, demands energy. Argument, justification, and choice are a waste of energy, and therefore one never dies to the many yesterdays so that the mind can be made fresh and new. When once there is the clarity of self-knowing, then love with its gentleness follows; there comes a spontaneous quality of humility, and also this freedom from the past through death.

And out of all this comes creation. Creation is not self-expression, it is not a matter of putting paint on a piece of canvas, or writing a few or many words in the form of a book, or making bread in the kitchen, or conceiving a child. None of that is creation. There is creation only when there is love and death. Creation can come only when there is a dying every day to everything, so that there is no accumulation as memory. Obviously you must have a little accumulation in the way of your clothing, a house, and personal property, I am not talking about that. It is the mind's inward sense of accumulation and possession—from which arise domination, authority, conformity, obedience—that prevents creation, because such a mind is never free. Only a free mind knows what death is and what love is; and for that mind alone there is creation. In this state, the mind is religious. In this state there is sacredness.

To me the word *sacredness* has an extraordinary meaning. Please, I am not doing propaganda for that word, I am not seeking to convince you of anything, and I am not trying to make you feel or experience reality through that word. You can't. You have to go through all this for yourself, not verbally, but actually. You actually have to die to everything you know, to your memories, to your miseries, to your pleasures. And when there is no jealousy, no envy, no greed, no torture of despair, then you will know what love is, and you will come upon that which may be called sacred. Therefore sacredness is the essence of religion. You know, a great river may become polluted as it flows past a town, but if the pollution isn't too great the river cleanses itself as it goes along, and within a few miles it is again clean, fresh, pure. Similarly, when once the mind comes upon this sacredness, then every act is a cleansing act. Through its very movement the mind is making itself innocent, and therefore it is not accumulating. A mind that has discovered this sacredness is in constant revolution, not economic or social revolution, but an inner revolution through which it is endlessly purifying itself. Its action is not based on some idea or formula. As the river with a tremendous volume of water behind it cleanses itself as it flows, so does the mind cleanse itself when once it has come upon this religious sacredness.

From The Ending of Time,
2 April 1980

Krishnamurti: You are a scientist, you have examined the atom, and so on. Don't you, when you have examined all that, feel there is something much more, beyond all that?

David Bohm: You can always feel that there is more beyond that, but it doesn't tell you what it is. It is clear that whatever one knows is limited.

K: Yes.

DB: And there must be more beyond.

K: How can that communicate with you, so that you, with your scientific knowledge, with your brain capacity, can grasp it?

DB: Are you saying it can't be grasped?

K: No. How can you grasp it? I don't say you can't grasp it. Can you grasp it?

DB: Look, it is not clear. You were saying before that it is ungraspable by . . .

K: Grasp, in the sense, can your mind go beyond theories? What I am trying to say is, can you move into it? Not move, in the sense of time and all that. Can you enter it? No, those are all words. What is beyond emptiness? Is it silence?

DB: Isn't that similar to emptiness?

K: Yes, that is what I am getting at. Move step by step. Is it silence? Or is silence part of emptiness?

DB: Yes, I should say that.

K: I should say that too. If it is not silence, could we—I am just asking—could we say it is something absolute? You understand?

DB: Well, we could consider the absolute. It would have to be something totally independent; that is what 'absolute' really means. It doesn't depend on anything.

K: Yes. You are getting somewhere near it.

DB: Entirely self-moving, as it were, self-active.

K: Yes. Would you say everything has a cause, and that has no cause at all?

DB: You see, this notion is already an old one. This notion has been developed by Aristotle, that this absolute is the cause of itself.

K: Yes.

DB: It has no cause, in a sense. That is the same thing.

K: You see the moment you said Aristotle—it is not that. How shall we get at this? Emptiness is energy, and that emptiness exists in silence, or the other way round, it doesn't matter—right? Oh, yes, there is something beyond all this. Probably it can never be put into words. But it must be put into words. You follow?

DB: You are saying that the absolute must be put into words, but we feel it can't be? Any attempt to put it into words makes it relative.

K: Yes. I don't know how to put all this.

DB: I think that we have a long history of danger with the absolute. People have put it in words, and it has become very oppressive.

K: Leave all that. You see, being ignorant of what other people have said, Aristotle and the Buddha, and so on, has an advantage. You understand what I mean? An advantage in the sense that the mind is not coloured by other people's ideas, not caught in other people's statements. All that is part of our conditioning. Now, to go beyond all that! What are we trying to do?

DB: I think, to communicate regarding this absolute, this beyond.

K: I took away that word *absolute* immediately.

DB: Then whatever it is; the beyond emptiness and silence.

K: Beyond all that. There is beyond all that. All that is something, part of an immensity.

DB: Yes, well even the emptiness and silence is an immensity, isn't it? The energy is itself an immensity.

K: Yes, I understand that. But there is something much more immense than that. Emptiness and silence and energy are immense, really immeasurable. But there is something—I am using the word, *greater*, than that.

DB: I am just considering. I am looking at it. One can see that whatever you say about emptiness, or about any other thing, there is something beyond.

K: No, as a scientist, why do you accept—not accept, forgive me for using that word—why do you even move along with this?

DB: Because we have come this far step by step, seeing the necessity of each step.

K: You see all that is very logical, reasonable, sane.

DB: And also, one can see that it is so right.

K: Yes. So if I say there is something greater than all this silence, energy—would you accept that? Accept in the sense that up to now we have been logical.

DB: We will say that whatever you speak of there is certainly something beyond it. Silence, energy, whatever, then there is always room logically for something beyond that. But the point is this: that even if you were to say there is something beyond that, still you logically leave room for going again beyond that.

K: No.

DB: Well why is that? You see, whatever you say, there is always room for something beyond.

K: There is nothing beyond.

DB: Well that point is not clear, you see.

K: There is nothing beyond it. I stick to that. Not dogmatically or obstinately. I feel that is the beginning and the ending of everything. The ending and the beginning are the same—right?

DB: In which sense? In the sense that you are using the beginning of everything as the ending?

K: Yes. Right? You would say that?

DB: Yes. If we take the ground from which it comes, it must be the ground to which it falls.

K: That's right. That is the ground upon which everything exists, space . . .

DB: . . . energy . . .

K: . . . energy, emptiness, silence, all that is. All that. Not ground, you understand?

DB: No, it is just a metaphor.

K: There is nothing beyond it. No cause. If you have a cause then you have ground.

DB: You have another ground.

K: No. That is the beginning and the ending.

DB: It is becoming more clear.

K: That's right. Does that convey anything to you?

DB: Yes, well I think that it conveys something.

K: Something. Would you say further, there is no beginning and no ending?

DB: Yes. It comes from the ground, goes to the ground, but it does not begin or end.

K: Yes. There is no beginning and no ending. The implications are enormous. Is that death—not death in the sense, I will die, but the complete ending of everything?

DB: You see at first you said that the emptiness is the ending of everything, so in what sense is this more, now? Emptiness is the ending of things, isn't it?

K: Yes, yes. Is that death, this emptiness? Death of everything the mind has cultivated. This emptiness is not the product of the mind, of the particular mind.

DB: No, it is the universal mind.

K: That emptiness is that.

DB: Yes.

K: That emptiness can only exist when there is death—total death—of the particular.

DB: Yes.

K: I don't know if I am conveying this.

DB: Yes, that is the emptiness. But then you are saying that, in this ground, death goes further?

K: Oh, yes.

DB: So we are saying the ending of the particular, the death of the particular, is the emptiness, which is universal. Now are you going to say that the universal also dies?

K: Yes, that is what I am trying to say.

DB: Into the ground.

K: Does it convey anything?

DB: Possibly, yes.

K: Just hold it a minute. Let's see it. I think it conveys something, doesn't it?

DB: Yes. Now if the particular and the universal die, then that is death?

K: Yes. After all, an astronomer says everything in the universe is dying, exploding, dying.

DB: But of course you could suppose that there was something beyond.

K: Yes, that is just it.

DB: I think we are moving. The universal and the particular. First the particular dies into the emptiness, and then comes the universal.

K: And that dies too.

DB: Into the ground, right?

K: Yes.

DB: So you could say the ground is neither born nor dies.

K: That's right.

DB: Well, I think it becomes almost inexpressible if you say the universal is gone, because expression is the universal.

K: You see—I am just explaining—everything is dying, except that. Does this convey anything?

DB: Yes. Well it is out of that that everything arises and into which it dies.

K: So that has no beginning and no ending.

DB: What would it mean to talk of the ending of the universal? What would it mean to have the ending of the universal?

K: Nothing. Why should it have a meaning if it is happening? What has that to do with man? You follow what I mean? Man who is going through a terrible time. What has that got to do with man?

DB: Let's say that man feels he must have some contact with the ultimate ground in his life, otherwise there is no meaning.

K: But it hasn't. That ground hasn't any relationship with man. He is killing himself, he is doing everything contrary to the ground.

DB: Yes, that is why life has no meaning for man.

K: I am an ordinary man; I say, all right, you have talked marvellously of sunsets, but what has that got to do with me? Will that or your talk help me to get over my ugliness? My quarrels with my wife or whatever it is?

DB: I think I would go back and say, we went into this logically starting from the suffering of mankind, showing it originates in a wrong turning, that leads inevitably . . .

K: Yes, but man asks, help me to get past the wrong turn. Put me on the right path. And to that one says, please don't become anything.

DB: Right. What is the problem then?

K: He won't even listen.

DB: Then it seems to me that it is necessary for the one who sees this to find out what is the barrier to listening.

K: Obviously you can see what is the barrier.

DB: What is the barrier?

K: 'I.'

DB: Yes, but I meant more deeply.

K: More deeply, all your thoughts, deep attachments—all that is in your way. If you can't leave these, then you will have no relationship with that. But man doesn't want to leave these.

DB: Yes, I understand. What he wants is the result of the way he is thinking.

K: What he wants is some comfortable, easy way of living without any trouble, and he can't have that.

DB: No. Only by dropping all this.

K: There must be a connection. There must be some relationship with the ground and this, some relationship with ordinary man. Otherwise, what is the meaning of living?

DB: That is what I was trying to say before. Without this relationship . . .

K: . . . there is no meaning.

DB: And then people invent meaning.

K: Of course.

DB: Even going back, the ancient religions have said similar things, that God is the ground, so they say seek God, you know.

K: Ah, no, this isn't God.

DB: No, it is not God, but it is saying the same. You could say that 'God' is an attempt to put this notion a bit too personally perhaps.

K: Yes. Give them hope, give them faith, you follow? Make life a little more comfortable to live.

DB: Well, are you asking at this point: how is this to be conveyed to the ordinary man? Is that your question?

K: More or less. And also it is important that he should listen to this. You are a scientist. You are good enough to listen because we are friends. But who will listen among the other scientists? I feel that if one pursues this we will have a marvellously ordered world.

DB: Yes. And what will we do in this world?

K: Live.

DB: But, I mean, we said something about creativity . . .

K: Yes. And then if you have no conflict, no 'I', there is something else operating.

DB: Yes, it is important to say that, because the Christian idea of perfection may seem rather boring because there is nothing to do!

K: We must continue this some other time, because it is something that has got to be put into orbit.

DB: It seems impossible.

K: We have gone pretty far.

From Krishnamurti's Notebook

27 June 1961

FORMULATION AND WORDS about all this seem so futile; words however accurate, however clear the description, do not convey the real thing.

There's a great and unutterable beauty in all this. There is only one movement in life, the outer and the inner; this movement is indivisible, though it is divided. Being divided, most follow the outer movement of knowledge, ideas, beliefs, authority, security, prosperity, and so on. In reaction to this, one follows the so-called inner life, with its visions, hopes, aspirations, secrecies, conflicts, despairs. As this movement is a reaction, it is in conflict with the outer. So there is contradiction, with its aches, anxieties, and escapes.

There is only one movement, which is the outer and the inner. With the understanding of the outer, then the inner movement begins, not in opposition or in contradiction. As conflict is eliminated, the brain, though highly sensitive and alert, becomes quiet. Then only the inner movement has validity and significance.

Out of this movement there is a generosity and compassion that is not the outcome of reason and purposeful self-denial.

The flower is strong in its beauty as it can be forgotten, set aside, or destroyed.

The ambitious do not know beauty. The feeling of essence is beauty.

28 June 1961

That which is sacred has no attributes. A stone in a temple, an image in a church, a symbol is not sacred. Man calls them sacred, something holy to be worshipped out of complicated urges, fears, and longings. This 'sacredness' is still within the field of thought; it is built up by thought and in thought there's nothing new or holy. Thought can put together the intricacies of systems, dogmas, beliefs, and the images, symbols it projects are no more holy than the blueprints of a house or the design of a new airplane. All this is within the frontiers of thought and there is nothing sacred or mystical about all this. Thought is matter and it can be made into anything, ugly or beautiful.

But there is a sacredness that is not of thought, nor of a feeling resuscitated by thought. It is not recognizable by thought nor can it be utilized by thought. Thought cannot formulate it. But there is a sacredness, untouched by any symbol or word. It is not communicable. It is a fact.

A fact is to be seen and the seeing is not through the word. When a fact is interpreted, it ceases to be a fact; it becomes something entirely different. The seeing is of the highest importance. This seeing is out of time-space; it's immediate, instantaneous. And what's seen is never the same again. There's no again or in the meantime.

This sacredness has no worshipper, the observer who meditates upon it. It's not in the market to be bought or sold. Like beauty, it cannot be seen through its opposite for it has no opposite.

That presence is here, filling the room, spilling over the hills, beyond the waters, covering the earth.

Sources and Acknowledgments

From the verbatim report of the fifth public talk in Bombay, 6 January 1960, in *Collected Works of J. Krishnamurti*, © 1992 Krishnamurti Foundation of America.

From the authentic report of the first public talk in Eddington, Pennsylvania, 12 June 1936, in *Collected Works of J. Krishnamurti*, © 1991 Krishnamurti Foundation of America.

From *Talks in Europe 1967*, London, 30 September 1967, © 1968 The Krishnamurti Foundation London.

From the verbatim report of the first public talk in Seattle, 16 July 1950, in *Collected Works of J. Krishnamurti*, © 1991 Krishnamurti Foundation of America.

From *Talks in Europe 1967*, Paris, 30 April 1967, © 1968 The Krishnamurti Foundation London

From chapter 28 of *The First and Last Freedom*, © 1987 Krishnamurti Foundation of America.

From chapter 4 of *Life Ahead*, © 1963 Krishnamurti Writings, Inc.

From chapter 7 of *Life Ahead*, © 1963 Krishnamurti Writings, Inc.

From chapter 18 of *Commentaries on Living First Series*, © 1956 Krishnamurti Writings, Inc.

From the authentic report of the seventh public talk in Bombay, 3 March 1965, in *Collected Works of J. Krishnamurti*, © 1992 Krishnamurti Foundation of America.

From the verbatim report of the first public talk in Bangalore, 4 July 1948, in *Collected Works of J. Krishnamurti*, © 1991 Krishnamurti Foundation of America.

From the verbatim report of the fourth public talk in Bombay, 8 February 1948, in *Collected Works of J. Krishnamurti*, © 1991 Krishnamurti Foundation of America.

From the verbatim report of the fourth public talk in Bombay, 27 February 1955, in *Collected Works of J. Krishnamurti*, © 1991 Krishnamurti Foundation of America.

From the verbatim report of the ninth public talk in Bombay, 24 December 1958, in *Collected Works of J. Krishnamurti*, © 1992 Krishnamurti Foundation of America.

From the verbatim report of the eighth public talk in Bombay, 8 March 1961, in *Collected Works of J. Krishnamurti*, © 1992 Krishnamurti Foundation of America.

From the verbatim report of the fourth public talk in London, 23 October 1949, in *Collected Works of J. Krishnamurti*, © 1991 Krishnamurti Foundation of America.

From the verbatim report of the sixth public talk at Madras, 29 January 1964, in *Collected Works of J. Krishnamurti*; © 1992 Krishnamurti Foundation of America.

From the transcript of the tape recording of the fourth public talk at Madras, 15 December 1974, © 1991 Krishnamurti Foundation Trust, Ltd.

From *Krishnamurti's Notebook*, 20 July 1961, © 1976 Krishnamurti Foundation Trust, Ltd.

From the verbatim report of the sixth public talk in New Delhi, 31 October 1956, in *Collected Works of J. Krishnamurti*, © 1992 Krishnamurti Foundation of America.

From the verbatim report of the sixth public talk at Ojai, 5 July 1953, in *Collected Works of J. Krishnamurti*, © 1991 Krishnamurti Foundation of America.

From the verbatim report of the sixth public talk at Ojai, 21 August 1955, in *Collected Works of J. Krishnamurti*, © 1992 Krishnamurti Foundation of America.

From the verbatim report of the questions following the sixth public talk at Ojai, 21 August 1955, in *Collected Works of J. Krishnamurti*, © 1992 Krishnamurti Foundation of America.

From the authentic report of the tenth public talk at Saanen, 2 August 1964, in *Collected Works of J. Krishnamurti*, © 1991 Krishnamurti Foundation of America.

From the authentic report of the tenth public talk at Saanen, 1 August 1965, in *Collected Works of J. Krishnamurti*, © 1992 Krishnamurti Foundation of America.

From *The Ending of Time*, 2 April 1980, © 1985 Krishnamurti Foundation Trust, Ltd.

From *Krishnamurti's Notebook*, 27 June 1961, © 1976 Krishnamurti Foundation Trust, Ltd.